CECIL POOLE

ALSO BY JAMES HASKINS

The Day Martin Luther King, Jr., Was Shot
Rosa Parks: My Story, with Rosa Parks
Thurgood Marshall: A Life for Justice
The Scottsboro Boys

CECIL POOLE
A LIFE IN THE LAW

JAMES HASKINS

NINTH JUDICIAL CIRCUIT HISTORICAL SOCIETY
PASADENA, CALIFORNIA

Library of Congress Cataloguing-in-Publication Data

Haskins, James, 1941–
    Cecil Poole : a life in the law / James Haskins.
    p. cm.
    Includes bibliographical references and index.
    Summary: Describes the life of Cecil Poole, the first African American U.S. attorney
    in the continental United States and the first black judge of the U.S. District Court
    for the Northern District of California.
    ISBN 0-9635086-2-8
    1. Poole, Cecil F., 1914–   . 2. African American judges—California—Biography—Juvenile
    literature. 3. African American lawyers—California—Biography—Juvenile literature. [1. Poole,
    Cecil F., 1914–   . 2. Lawyers. 3. Judges. 4. African Americans—Biography.]   I. Title.
    KF373.P66.H37 2002
    340'.092—dc21
    [B]

    2002010871

Edited by Judith Forman
Index by Barbara Wilcie Kern
Book design by Matthew Williams

DEDICATION

This book is dedicated to
Nicholle Charlotte Allair
and a future filled with promise,
and to her mother, Patti Poole.

Thanks

This book was made possible in part by the generous support of the following:

Columbia Foundation

De Goff & Sherman Foundation

Levi Strauss Company

van Loben Sels Foundation

Walter & Elise Haas Fund

U.S. District Court,
 Northern District of California

Richard & Rhoda Goldman Fund

Evelyn & Walter Haas, Jr. Fund

Koret Foundation

Sidney Stern Memorial Trust

Coblentz, Patch, Duffy & Bass

Sheppard, Mullin,
 Richter & Hampton

Hafif Family Foundation

Kazan, McClain, Edises,
 Simon & Abrams Foundation

Aaron H. Braun

Jerome I. Braun, Esq.

Brobeck, Phleger & Harrison

James J. Brosnahan, Esq.

K. Louise Francis, Esq.

Hon. Procter Hug, Jr.

W. Douglas Kari, Esq.

Mr. & Mrs. William Lowenstein

McCutchen, Doyle, Brown & Enersen

Morrison & Foerster Foundation

Laurence Myers

National Urban League

Norman H. Ruecker

Mr. & Mrs. Harold Zlot

We gratefully acknowledge the support of all the contributors.

TABLE OF CONTENTS

Acknowledgments

I AM GRATEFUL TO THE MANY CONTRIBUTORS TO THE JUDGE Poole Biography Project and especially to Jerome I. Braun, Esq., chairman of the NJCHS Judge Poole Biography Project, and Bradley B. Williams, director/editor, Ninth Judicial Circuit Historical Society. Special thanks are due Victoria DeGoff, whose initial generosity inspired so many others. Of invaluable aid were the interviews of Judge Poole conducted by Carole Hicke in 1993 and published as *Civil Rights, Law, and the Federal Courts: The Life of Cecil Poole, 1914–1997* by The Regents of the University of California in 1997 as part of the Northern California U.S. District Court Oral History Series.

Also of great help were the reminiscences of Poole's daughter, Patti, and of the many colleagues, friends, acquaintances, and staff of Cecil F. Poole. In alphabetical order, they are Tom Berkley, Meredith Blain, Mayor Willie Brown, Judge James Browning, William K. Coblentz, Victoria De Goff, Judge Terry J. Hatter, Judge Thelton Henderson, Judge Procter Hug, Judge Lowell Jensen, Jerrold Ladar, Judge Charles A. Legge, Debbie McIntyre, Fred Morsell, Susan Newell, Judge Marilyn Patel, Judge Stephen Reinhardt, Judge Charles Renfrew, Jerome J. Shestach, Judge Mary Schroeder, Judge William Shubb, Judge William Schwarzer, Irma Smith, Judge Fern M. Smith, Judge Joseph T. Sneed, Judge Jack E. Tanner, and Jayne Williams.

During my visits to the West Coast, Catherine Todd, Melanie Moore, and Jeanne Wong were of invaluable assistance in seeing me through airports and hotel rooms, making travel and lodging arrangements, and setting up countless interview appointments. Christine Vargas and Jennifer Noughton spent hours transcribing interview tapes. Kathy Benson helped put it all together.

INTRODUCTION

FOR ALMOST FIFTY YEARS, I KNEW THE BOUNTY OF CECIL POOLE'S friendship and compassion. We first became acquainted when he began his career in California working for the federal government. But it was not until Cecil joined the San Francisco district attorney's office, then headed by future governor Edmund G. "Pat" Brown, that our friendship blossomed.

Cecil and his charming wife, Charlotte, were friends of my wife, Jean, and me, and we saw each other on many occasions. When Cecil and I accepted positions in Sacramento to work with newly elected Governor Brown, we were reluctant at that time to move our families. So we shared an apartment for almost a year, and during that time we got to know each other very well.

I found during that time that Cecil had the courage to speak plainly when that was right and needed, and the everlasting intuition and tact to be silent when that would prove the sovereign remedy. He indeed looked at the world with a steady gaze.

Cecil was a man of values, high ones. I know he held onto the values of the past provisionally only in the knowledge that they would change, but he held them as guides. This was not, as Justice Oliver Wendell Holmes once remarked, a duty; it was a necessity. How else are we to know anything?

Cecil loved to talk history, law, historic personalities. He was at special pains to know thoroughly those personalities he had most reason to distrust or deplore. Or, to quote his brother-in-spirit, the British political writer and statesman Edmund Burke, persons who lacked "what I call principles, a uniform rule and scheme of life."

Cecil never commented on a court decision, whether it was the Supreme Court's, his own, or that of another court of appeals, without having the text before him. He had to know the fine points. But when he had them clearly in mind, he moved quickly. His judgment was firm and unformed by fashion. He was high minded, but high-mindedness floating free of facts made him squirm. He did not hesitate to commit himself for fear of later reversal. It did not matter if an opinion had to be changed. The only abiding thing, as the late United States Supreme Court Justice Louis Brandeis used to repeat, is change.

Cecil and I spent time together in a lot of places, most of them respectable and not all of them easy. One thing you can say about Cecil—he could talk in depth on any subject, and he sometimes did. He was as good on foreign relations as he was on legal principles. This is known as the unrevealing comparative.

Cecil gave me and many others wisdom, generosity of spirit, respect, fairness, compassion, and brotherhood. He believed in the words of Huddie Ledbetter, the immortal minstrel of Morinsport, Louisiana: "We are in the same boat, brother, and when you shake one end, you gonna rock the other."

William K. Coblentz, Esq.
San Francisco

CHAPTER 1

"BEST SHOW I HAD EVER SEEN"

WHEN CECIL POOLE WAS ABOUT FOURTEEN YEARS OLD, HE found himself in a big city courthouse. His father was involved in a legal dispute over money, and Cecil went with him to court.

"It looked like everything was built for giants," said Cecil of the imposing courtroom many years later. His father's attorney, William G. Stanton, was anything but a giant. In fact, he was a small man. But he acted big. He strutted around the courtroom, making dramatic, expansive gestures. His voice boomed out. Cecil loved to hear him cry out, "I object, Your Honor!"

"Best show I had ever seen in my life," said Poole.

Young Cecil Poole was full of questions for Stanton. Pleased with the youngster's interest, Stanton offered to take him to other trials. Soon Cecil had decided that he, too, wanted to be a trial lawyer. In spite of the barriers to blacks in any profession in America during most of the twentieth century, he achieved his goal. Later he became the first black assistant district attorney in San Francisco, California. He went on to become the first black executive clemency secretary for a California governor, the first black American in the continental United States to be named a United States attorney, and the first black district court judge in northern California. He capped his career by becoming only the second black judge on the U.S. Court of Appeals for the Ninth Circuit.

This is Judge Cecil Poole's story. Through the lens of his life, it is also a view of the United States of America during the twentieth century. Much of the history of the nation in that century concerned the way American law adapted and changed to conform more closely to the promise on which the nation was founded. In particular, it was a century during which black Americans were finally accepted as full citizens on the basis of a document written two centuries earlier: the United States Constitution. What Poole brought to the law, and to his America, was a deep and abiding sense that the law existed to serve the people of the United States. He understood that, while law is necessary to determine the relationships between people, it is important not to lose sight of people when determining the law.

Cecil Poole, about age 18

CHAPTER 2

THE POOLES
MOVE NORTH

CECIL FRANCIS POOLE WAS BORN ON JULY 25, 1914, JUST A MONTH after the start of World War I. By the end of that summer, all of Europe was embroiled in the largest war the world had yet seen. At first, the United States remained neutral in the conflict between Germany and its allies and Great Britain, France, and theirs. After German submarines sank the British ocean liner *Lusitania* in the spring of 1916, the tide of U.S. public opinion began to turn. On April 6, 1917, President Woodrow Wilson announced U.S. entry into the war "to make the world safe for democracy." Backed by the almost unlimited resources and manpower of the United States, the Allies were victorious. Germany surrendered in November 1918, and the United States emerged as a major world power.

Cecil Poole's father, William Thomas Poole, did not serve in the U.S. military. Blacks were not particularly welcome in the segregated military services. The 400,000 black Americans who did enlist or were drafted represented about 10 percent of the U.S. forces. They were mostly from the North. Only about 50,000 actually saw combat. The vast majority worked in labor battalions, loading and unloading ships, building fortifications, burying the battlefield dead. White American officers generally hated and scorned black troops under their command. In Birmingham, Alabama, where the Pooles lived, few blacks dared to enlist. It was too manly a thing to do in a region where the entire social and legal structure was dedicated to denying humanity to blacks.

Although Cecil Poole's parents, William and Eva, were thus spared the family disruption war can cause, they did not escape another tragedy of the World War I years—a severe flu epidemic. The mysterious malady that came to be called Spanish influenza struck first at Fort Riley, Kansas, on March 11, 1918. Within a week, five hundred soldiers had come down with the virus. Soon outbreaks were being reported in other parts of the country, and by the middle of October the killer virus had claimed nearly two hundred thousand lives. The next month, when crowds gathered in public places to celebrate the end of World War I, many wore facemasks to avoid falling victim to the worst epidemic in American history.

By the time the flu disappeared as mysteriously as it had come, some 675,000 Americans were dead—a number larger than all the American casualties in all the wars of the twentieth century combined. Among the victims was one of the Poole children. Cecil Poole was only four years old at the time—too young to remember the tragedy. The baby of the family, he would grow up with two older siblings— Marjorie Ellen and William, Jr.—rather than three.

The world in which little Cecil Poole spent his first years was a stranger to the democracy that President Wilson had vowed to defend when he announced U.S. entry into World War I. Segregation reigned in Alabama and elsewhere in the Deep South. Slavery may have been outlawed after the North won the Civil War, but across the South many blacks lived in virtual slavery as sharecroppers on farms owned by whites. Blamed for the Civil War and the loss of the "southern way of life" when the Confederacy was vanquished, blacks were separated from whites in almost every area of life. By law, the Poole children had to play in separate areas of public parks. Like other blacks, the Pooles could drink water only from public fountains marked "Colored." When they traveled on the city's street railway, they had to sit in separate cars or sections designated for blacks.

Side by side with the laws of segregation in the South, there existed the customs of separation. When Eva Poole took her children shopping in a white-owned clothing store, she could not let them try on anything. White customers refused even to touch, let alone buy, an item of clothing or a pair of shoes that had been worn by blacks. When William Poole paid for a purchase at a white-owned store, he could not hand his money directly to a clerk. He had to put the cash on the counter, and pick up change from the same place. If he passed a white person on a sidewalk, he had to lower his eyes—or even step off into the street to allow the white person to pass.

Blacks could be arrested for sitting in the white section of a streetcar or drinking from a "Whites Only" water fountain. But far more frightening than arrest was the brutal punishment of the vigilante "justice" that existed side by side with the formal, institutionalized system of written laws and courts. Once legal slavery ended after the Civil War, defenders of slavery formed groups whose purpose was to keep blacks down, often by vigilante, or extra-legal, means. The most famous of these groups was the Ku Klux Klan, which was committed to white supremacy and was also virulently anti-Catholic and anti-Jewish. Claiming to be defenders of Protestant faith, the Klan seized upon the most sacred Christian symbol, the cross, as an emblem of its cause. By setting a cross on fire, Klansmen turned it into a weapon of terror and hatred, designed to intimidate and frighten blacks.

The Klan and other white supremacist groups also used deliberate racial murder and lynching. Although illegal mob killings of blacks were on the decline by the time Cecil Poole was born in 1914, favorite Klan practices like night riding and cross burning increased as lynching subsided.

Birmingham, Alabama, where the Pooles lived, was a center of Klan activity. The Klan's targets were often labor unionists whose efforts to organize steel and coal industry workers threatened the choke-hold that the city's business and political leaders held on those industries. Local law enforcement, instead of enforcing the law, sustained injustice. Most whites in Birmingham had ties to the Klan, although they did not all engage in Klan terror. They were referred to as "Klan plus" or "Klan minus," depending on their willingness to murder people.

Most blacks were not employed in the coal and steel industries and so avoided direct involvement in the labor clashes that were so much a part of Birmingham life in the teens and twenties. William Poole's family operated a funeral home—a steady business in a region with separate mortuaries and cemeteries for blacks. Rather than enter the family business, William Poole had chosen to attend normal school and become a teacher. Eva Poole had also gone to normal school, which offered two years of training after high school. Few blacks went to four-year colleges.

Teaching was one of the few professions open to black people, and teachers were highly respected in the black community. In fact, William and Eva Poole would have been counted among the members of the "Talented Tenth." A term coined by black educator and author W.E.B. Du Bois, it referred to the most able 10 percent of black Americans—teachers, professional men, ministers, and spokesmen. William Poole was an assistant principal at an elementary school in Birmingham. Eva Poole taught for a short time before their children were born.

The respect of the black community for its teachers was not shared by the whites of Birmingham, who didn't think blacks needed schooling. William Poole was supposed to be grateful for what few resources his school was given and was not to ask for new textbooks or heated school buildings. He was expected to follow curriculum established by the white school board, which meant teaching black children that their only history was slavery. But there was a long tradition of subversion in black schools. They displayed portraits of great, historic black leaders on bulletin boards when it was safe, and swiftly removed them when a white school board member visited. Outraged by the unequal treatment his students and fellow teachers suffered, William Poole had the courage to express his indignation to the superintendent of Birmingham's schools. According to Cecil Poole, after one such argument with the superintendent, his father packed up the family and left Birmingham altogether and moved to Pittsburgh, Pennsylvania.

It is likely that the Pooles would have moved anyway, even if William Poole had managed to get along with his superintendent.

Since the 1890s, educated southern blacks had been leaving the South in ever-increasing numbers, convinced that there were few opportunities for them in the former slave states. The years surrounding World War I simply presented more reasons to move. The Deep South experienced a major economic downturn, from which blacks suffered more than whites. In 1915 floods and boll weevil infestations of cotton crops made it impossible for most black sharecroppers and other farm workers to make a living. During World War I, even before the United States officially entered the conflict, U.S. industries were major suppliers of war materiel to the Allies in Europe. The booming war industries in the North were starved for labor. Due to restrictive immigration laws and the return of many immigrants to fight for their European homelands, for the first time in decades there were not enough white immigrant workers for the available jobs. Desperate factory owners began hiring blacks, and more and more southern blacks migrated to the northern cities.

William Poole's brother had earlier moved to Pittsburgh, Pennsylvania. Coincidentally, Pittsburgh was a center of the steel industry, like Birmingham. Pittsburgh's black population was growing fast, and Cecil Poole's uncle saw his opportunity to open a branch of the family funeral home. Often, after one member of a family migrated north and settled in, others joined him or her. Following that pattern, William Poole moved his family north to Pittsburgh not long after his brother. Most blacks with the means to get out of the South did so in this era of black movement north called the Great Migration. Two other brothers of William Poole moved to Chicago with their families.

Cecil was about four years old when the William Poole family boarded a train for Pittsburgh. He remembered little about the trip other than sleeping on the train seat with his mother's fur coat for a blanket and being met at the Pittsburgh station by his aunt and uncle.

When the Pooles arrived in Pittsburgh, the city's black community was growing rapidly. The cutoff of European immigration because of World War I forced employers in the steel, iron, and glass industries to hire blacks for the first time, and southern blacks flocked to the city, more than doubling its black population by 1940. These migrants brought new energy and creativity to Pittsburgh. Robert Vann, born in North Carolina, founded the *Pittsburgh Courier* in 1910. Twenty years later, when Cecil Poole was sixteen years old, the *Courier* was the black newspaper with the largest circulation in the country. Migrants also filled the team roster of the Homestead Grays, one of the best Negro League baseball teams, organized in Pittsburgh six years before the Poole family arrived. By 1931, when Cecil Poole was in high school, black Pittsburgh proudly fielded a second Negro League team, the famous Pittsburgh Crawfords, whose eventual Hall of Famers would include Satchel Paige and Josh Gibson.

Most blacks settled in the hills surrounding central Pittsburgh. There was not enough room in the Hill District, however, for the large wave of new arrivals, so the black migrants spread throughout the city. The Pooles lived in integrated neighborhoods, side by side with European immigrants, and the Poole children attended integrated schools.

William Poole did not resume his teaching career in Pittsburgh. It was very difficult for a black teacher to get a job—especially if he was from the South and had only a normal school education and no college degree. So William Poole went into the mortuary business with his brother. As he got older, Cecil was embarrassed about the kind of work his father did for a living. Asked what work his father did, Cecil tended to say simply that the elder Poole "went into business."

Although it was not a source of pride for Cecil Poole, the family mortuary business provided a needed service: helping people who had lost relatives or friends to bury them with dignity. It was also a profitable business, which enabled the Pooles to live in comfort. The family moved several times within Pittsburgh during Cecil's growing-up years, each time to a larger home in a better neighborhood.

No matter where they lived, the Poole household was filled with music and books. Every Saturday, William Poole listened to radio broadcasts from the Metropolitan Opera in New York, and under his influence, Cecil developed a love for classical music, though with less enthusiasm for opera than his father. Marjorie Ellen, William, Jr., and Cecil all played musical instruments. All three learned to read before they entered school. Their parents taught them at home and also took them to story hours at the public library a few blocks away. Back in Birmingham, blacks had been barred from the public library.

Cecil entered kindergarten at William H. McElvey School in Pittsburgh. His teachers were white, but he had both white and black classmates. Although he already knew how to read, he had not yet learned to write, and he had trouble learning script. He slanted his letters backwards, which was strictly forbidden. Over time, he managed to learn acceptable penmanship, but he never could write the letter "F." For the rest of his life, when he wrote his full name, including his middle name or initial, he printed the "F." He wasn't much better at drawing.

Cecil also had trouble with math. He managed to learn addition and subtraction and to memorize the multiplication tables. But an understanding of the basic concepts eluded him. As his class started learning decimals and fractions, he began to fall seriously behind. Not only did he have trouble keeping up with the work, but he also started to feel self-conscious and dumb. Finally, one of his teachers suggested that his parents hire a math tutor for their son. The elder Pooles considered the money well spent if it would help Cecil improve in math. With the aid of the private tutor, Cecil managed to catch up with his class in math. But his difficulties would resurface in high school.

Bible teachings were part of the curriculum when Cecil was in school. He was in third grade when he began learning stories from the Old Testament. He loved the tales of war and strife, of battles and bloody fighting. He would go home and tell his father the stories, and his father would identify on a map the locations of various events. He also enjoyed battle poems and even, eighty years later, happily recited lines from *The Destruction of Semnacherib* by Lord Byron:

> *The Assyrian came down like the wolf on the fold,*
> *And his cohorts were gleaming in purple and gold;*
> *And the sheen of their spears were like stars on the sea,*
> *When the blue wave rolls nightly on deep Galilee.*

Cecil Poole was an active child. From an early age, he loved to run and had a reputation among his friends as the fastest runner. On weekends, William and Eva Poole took the children to local parks, where they could run around to their heart's content. Unlike parks in Birmingham, Pittsburgh's parks were integrated. The Poole family probably attended Negro League baseball games, not only in Pittsburgh but also perhaps in Chicago, Illinois, where the Negro League World Series was held every year. William Poole's two brothers and their families still lived in Chicago, and the Pooles would visit the Windy City for a week or more, staying with their relatives and seeing the sights. Once or twice, the Pooles went to a resort on a lake in the Pennsylvania Hills.

One year, Cecil's mother took a vacation by herself and brought back a Kodak camera for him. This proved to be the beginning of Cecil's lifelong interest in photography. Once the novice photographer took a picture of a little girl named Irma who lived up the street. Unfortunately, it did not come out. So Irma asked her father to take a picture of Cecil and her. She gave it to him, and Cecil kept it in his room. Eventually, he realized she had let him keep the photograph because she wasn't interested in it, or him.

In spite of that early disappointment, Cecil remained fascinated by photography. During high school, some of his shots were used in the school yearbook. Although there were black photographers who could have served as role models, including some in Pittsburgh, Cecil apparently never considered photography as a career. Friends and acquaintances remark on his constant picture taking and wonder why he didn't show them the developed photos. Perhaps that first attempt to capture his would-be girlfriend on film was formative: For Cecil, the act of photography was often more important than the pictures that resulted.

As he entered his teen years, Cecil began to think about his future career. He had no interest in joining his family's mortuary business. Most other career paths were essentially closed to him because he was black. He was as excited as every other thirteen-year-old boy when, in 1927, the aviator Charles Lindbergh flew his plane, *The Spirit of St. Louis*, nonstop from New York to Paris. Unlike white teenagers, however, Cecil could only dream of becoming a pilot. A white woman, Amelia Earhart, made a solo trans-Atlantic flight the year after Lindbergh. But the handful of black pilots in the United States could not get the financial backing to attempt such a feat.

Career possibilities were more open for blacks in the entertainment field. In fact, Pittsburgh was an active jazz center and cradled the talents of several great jazz artists who were Cecil Poole's contemporaries, including trumpet player Roy Eldridge, drummers Kenny Clarke and Art Blakey, composer-pianists Billy Strayhorn and Mary Lou Williams, and singers Lena Horne and Billy Eckstine. Cecil himself tried out the local music scene for a brief time, introduced to it by Billy Eckstine. Eckstine (he was born William Clarence Eckstein and would later change the spelling of his last name) was the same age as Cecil Poole, and the two were good friends as youngsters in Pittsburgh. One summer, Eckstine helped Poole get a job working with him on a garbage wagon. Already known for his fine voice and in demand to sing at parties, Eckstine formed a singing group, which Poole joined. But the older Pooles disapproved of the local nightlife that was centered at the intersection of Wylie and Fullerton Avenues in downtown Pittsburgh. The world of jazz music was rife with drugs, and Eva Poole persuaded Cecil to quit the group. Eckstine soon moved away from Pittsburgh with his family, relocating to Washington, D.C., where he completed high school.

Whatever lingering interest Cecil Poole might have had in a singing career was overshadowed by his life-changing experience in a Pittsburgh courtroom in his early high school years. That experience taught him that there was a strong element of performance in the soul of a trial lawyer. He would make his mark on the legal stage.

By the time Cecil Poole entered Pittsburgh's Schenley High School, his family lived in a large house with three floors and a basement. Cecil and his brother, William, Jr., had bedrooms on the third floor, where there was also a kind of family room filled with records and books. The house was close to the campus of the University of Pittsburgh. It was also only about half a mile from Schenley High School, so most of Cecil's neighborhood friends went there as well.

At Schenley High, Cecil took French and Latin, and after a couple of years was able to read Latin literature. He liked woodworking, played violin in the school orchestra, and worked on the yearbook. He was also on the track team and was one of its fastest runners. His tall, lean body sliced through the air and his long legs made yards seem like inches. He was careful about his appearance and cut a handsome figure, and his sense of humor made him popular among his friends and classmates. His troubles with math seemed to cast the only pall over those years. Algebra was a big problem for him. Fortunately, after-school tutoring was available at Schenley High. He also attended summer school one year in order to keep up with his class. Compared with the trouble he had with algebra, geometry was easy.

Cecil was fifteen and a sophomore at Schenley High School when the New York Stock Exchange crashed in the autumn of 1929. Farm prices had been depressed for several years before that, and industrial production had already slowed. Always "last hired and first fired," black Americans lost jobs in all economic sectors. After the Great Depression began in the early 1930s, black unemployment reached tragic rates, as high as 50 percent in industrial cities. In Philadelphia, it was a staggering 56 percent. Pittsburgh was a manufacturing center that depended on the steel and coal industries, both of which were severely affected by the Depression. Fortunately, the Pooles did not suffer as much as most blacks in the city. No matter what the economy, the undertaking business remains steady.

As the Great Depression wore on, labor union organizing increased, but blacks were virtually shut out of white labor unions. There was just one black labor union, the Brotherhood of Sleeping Car Porters, started by A. Philip Randolph in 1925. The Pooles knew a local labor union organizer, and young Cecil became aware of some of the issues between industry and labor, such as job security, working conditions, and the right of labor to make demands of employers and to strike if their demands were not met.

Cecil had more direct experience with the movement against racial segregation. His mother was active in the local chapter of the National Association for the Advancement of Colored People. The NAACP had been founded in 1909 by blacks (including W.E.B. Du Bois) and whites who wanted to work together to fight increasing white violence against black people, especially lynching in the South. The organization grew steadily in membership and influence, establishing local branches throughout the country. Cecil often accompanied his mother to meetings of the Pittsburgh branch of the NAACP. At first, he didn't really know or care what the meetings were about. By the time he was in high school, however, he had begun to pay attention.

Cecil now understood the reason why his parents had moved from Birmingham to Pittsburgh. They had done so to escape segregation and the racial violence that it fostered. Harder to understand was that segregation was legal—not just in the Deep South but throughout the United States. This was so in spite of the facts that the Declaration of Independence had proclaimed that "all men are created equal" and that the U.S. Constitution prohibited states from denying any citizen "the equal protection of the laws."

Legal segregation dated back to 1895. In that year, the United States Supreme Court had ruled in the case of *Plessy v. Ferguson* that separating the races was constitutional as long as the accommodations for both were equal. Over time, most states outside the South had chosen not to follow legal segregation. The reasons varied but were usually some combination of not having a strong history of slavery, not having a large black population, and believing that segregation was morally wrong. The states of the South had a different experience. They had long histories of slavery and had gone to war with the North in a vain attempt to preserve it. White southerners were determined to keep the blacks in their midst separate and powerless.

Listening at NAACP meetings, hearing his parents talk, and reading newspapers, Cecil Poole dreamed of one day making a difference in the lives of black people in America. His experience in court with his father's attorney showed him how he could.

Cecil had to get a college degree before he could enter law school. His father regarded only three predominantly white universities as worthy of consideration—University of Chicago, University of Michigan, and Harvard University. The Pooles' elder son, William, was attending the University of Michigan. On visits home, he told stories about the fun of college life, inspiring his younger brother to decide to go to Michigan, too. By the time Cecil enrolled there, however, his brother had transferred to the University of Iowa. Cecil

Poole set off for the University of Michigan in September 1932, at the height of the Great Depression. He remained there not only for the four years it took to earn his Bachelor of Arts degree but also for an additional two years of law school.

Charlotte Crump Poole, early 1940s

Cecil F. Poole, about age 25

CHAPTER 3

LOVE FOR THE LAW, LOVE OF HIS LIFE

BY THE TIME HE ENTERED THE UNIVERSITY OF MICHIGAN School of Law, Cecil Poole understood that "the law" was a very large and complicated body of rules governing nearly every aspect of life in society. A combination of local, state, and federal laws controls everything from whether and how many years one attends school to the age at which one can get a driver's license, vote, serve in the military, or get married. Drivers must obey traffic laws; homeowners must consider zoning and tax laws. The list is almost endless.

Cecil knew that lawyers (also called attorneys, counsels, counselors, solicitors, and advocates) give advice to clients, assist them in legal matters, and represent them in court. Some lawyers specialize in civil law, such as the attorney who represented Cecil's father in a dispute over money. Others specialize in criminal law, prosecuting or defending people accused of crimes like theft and murder.

At the time, black lawyers did not specialize in one kind of law or another; there were too few of them. They had to earn their living by taking many minor cases or preparing legal documents, like contracts and wills, for small fees. They were not highly regarded in the black community. In fact, some blacks preferred going to white lawyers, because they believed white attorneys could represent them better in the majority white justice system. Considering how racist that justice system was—especially in the segregated South—there really was a crying need for black lawyers with a passion for justice that did not discriminate. Slowly, such lawyers were beginning to emerge.

In 1929, Charles Hamilton Houston had joined the all-black Howard University Law School as vice dean. The law school had a poor reputation, but Houston devoted himself to strengthening enrollment standards, hiring better faculty, and introducing new courses. He concentrated on civil rights law, dreaming of training a group of young, bright, energetic black lawyers to attack unfair national, state, and local laws in the courts.

While Cecil Poole was still in college, his mother continued to work with the NAACP, and when he was home for summer vacations, Cecil would attend meetings with her. On one such occasion, she introduced him to Thurgood Marshall, a young attorney who had recently joined the organization and who was one of Houston's proteges. Fresh out of Howard University Law School, the tall, slim young man with the clipped mustache, booming voice, and wry sense of humor was concentrating on the NAACP's civil rights cases. Marshall traveled widely, especially in the South, to represent blacks who had been unfairly accused of crimes. He was also working with other NAACP lawyers to file legal suits seeking equal pay for southern black teachers.

As the Great Depression wore on, President Franklin D. Roosevelt and his administration attempted to spur a national recovery with a series of programs called the New Deal. The New Deal had two phases. The first (1933–34) tried to provide economic relief through programs of agricultural and business regulation, price stabilization, and public works. Soon acronyms like AAA and CCC were part of daily conversation. AAA stood for the Agricultural Adjustment Administration, which gave money to farmers in an attempt to halt falling prices of agricultural products caused by overproduction. CCC was the Civilian Conservation Corps, which hired unemployed men to build roads and work on irrigation and reforestation projects. These diverse programs held two things in common—their aim to bring about a national economic recovery and their almost total lack of black participation. Only a small percentage of black farmers, sharecroppers, and field hands received AAA subsidy checks. In its first two years, the CCC was 95 percent white. The TVA, or Tennessee Valley Authority, a New Deal program that built dams and hydroelectric generating stations in seven southern states, employed a massive labor force that was more than 99 percent white.

Through the congressional seniority system, southerners controlled the way New Deal program money was allocated. They were determined that blacks would benefit as little as possible. By the time Congress began to debate the codes regulating production, prices, wages, hours, and collective bargaining under the new National Recovery Administration (NRA), blacks were charging that the NRA stood for "Negroes Ruined Again."

The lack of opportunities for blacks in early New Deal programs extended to educated, professional blacks, including attorneys. As an example, Nelson H. Nichols, a young Washington, D.C., attorney, was accepted as a volunteer to explain the NRA to the average citizen. But when he applied for a paid position as an attorney with the NRA, he was told that NRA office positions were exclusively for whites.

Black leaders failed in their initial attempts to arrange a meeting with President Roosevelt. His closest advisers were southerners, who were certain he would lose the support of both Congress and white America if he so much as acknowledged the existence of black people. Those same advisers even banned black reporters from White House press conferences. Eventually, however, organized protests by black leaders, belated moves on the part of liberal whites in the government, and forceful lobbying of her husband by First Lady Eleanor Roosevelt brought about some changes.

Roosevelt named several blacks as special advisers, a group that came to be called the "Black Cabinet" or "Kitchen Cabinet." Some two dozen blacks were appointed to federal positions. They included Robert Vann, a lawyer who was also publisher-editor of the *Pittsburgh Courier*, as a special adviser in the Justice Department, and attorney William Hastie and Harvard-trained Ph.D. in economics Robert Weaver as assistant solicitor and special assistant at the U.S. Department of the Interior. Others received appointments at the National Recovery Administration and the U.S. Department of Commerce. Cecil Poole was euphoric. As he recalled many years later, "There were appointments being made of very high-grade professional black lawyers in positions where they had never been before. These were high old times. I'll never forget them."

Cecil wanted to join the growing number of attorneys in the federal government in Washington, D.C., but first he needed more schooling. After earning his law degree at the University of Michigan, he took the unusual step of earning a Master of Law degree— uncommon even for whites—at prestigious Harvard Law School. One of his professors was Felix Frankfurter, who would shortly be appointed the first Jewish associate justice on the United States Supreme Court. Poole was awed by Frankfurter's command of the law and delighted by the manner in which the professor handled the cheeky students who dared challenge him. Poole chuckled when he remembered, "He would call on somebody to answer a question, and three weeks later that guy's still answering the question."

Poole graduated from Harvard Law School in 1939. At last he was fully prepared to be the lawyer he had known he wanted to become more than a decade before. "There was nothing more that I wanted to do than to be a part of that New Deal Washington scene," he recalled. But that scene was already changing. The pace of New Deal programming had slackened as a result of Republican opposition. Then, on September 1, 1939, Germany invaded Poland, and in response, France and Great Britain declared war on Germany. For the second time in less than fifty years, Europe was at war. Although the United States was determined to remain neutral, its eyes were on Europe. The president and Congress were preoccupied with foreign affairs and not focused on domestic programs except as they related to the war.

Although he was anxious to work for the government, Poole had no connections in Washington. He returned to Pittsburgh and concentrated on gaining admittance to the Pennsylvania bar. Only then would he be eligible to practice law in Pennsylvania. Named for the rail that once enclosed the judge in a courtroom, in modern times the bar refers to a group of lawyers who are qualified to conduct trials of legal cases. Attorneys must be admitted to the bar before they can practice law in the United States. Each state has a bar, and the requirements for admission vary among the states. In general, they include having a law school degree and passing a state bar examination, which tests knowledge of the law of that particular state. To practice law in Pennsylvania, Poole had to pass the Pennsylvania bar exam. No matter what the state, many young attorneys failed the test the first time and had to retake it. Poole passed on his first attempt and was admitted to the Pennsylvania bar in 1940.

In those days, all new attorneys in Pennsylvania had to serve a six-month clerkship in addition to passing the bar. In this way, they would learn more about the precepts, or principles, of law. For a young black attorney, finding a law firm in which to clerk could be difficult. No white firm would hire a black clerk, and there were very few black law offices. In spite of its origins as a Quaker stronghold that outlawed slavery, Pennsylvania had been slow to admit black lawyers to practice. The state's first black lawyer, Jonathan Jasper Wright, had not been admitted until 1865, the year the Civil War ended. Even in Pittsburgh, black law practices were few. Poole served his clerkship with the top private black law partnership of Homer Brown and Richard Jones.

Homer S. Brown, born in West Virginia in 1896, had graduated from the University of Pittsburgh Law School and had formed a law partnership with his classmate, Richard F. Jones. He was president of the Pittsburgh NAACP, and would hold that office for a total of twenty-four years. In 1935, he had been elected to the Pennsylvania House of Representatives, where he would serve seven terms, authoring the state's fair employment practices act and leading a legislative investigation into hiring practices in Pittsburgh's public schools that resulted in the hiring of the first black teacher. In

November 1949, he became the first black judge elected to the County Court of Allegheny County, dispelling the claim that whites would not vote for a qualified black candidate.

In recalling his early career for a lengthy oral history, Poole made only brief mention of Brown and Jones law firm where he first clerked. He recalled that two other attorneys were with the firm when he arrived but that both soon left. Poole became an associate and was assigned the drudge work, like filing, copying documents, and keeping the case schedules for his two bosses. It would be quite a while before he had a chance to try a case in court.

While working for Brown and Jones, Poole received an invitation in the mail to join the American Bar Association. The ABA was and still is the main national organization of attorneys. It routinely invites new attorneys who pass the bar to join. Poole was skeptical when he looked at the official invitation. The ABA was a white organization that did not admit blacks. In fact, black lawyers had established a separate National Bar Association in the 1920s. But Poole looked at the information card and saw that there were boxes to be checked for different racial and ethnic categories. He took a chance and checked the box marked "Negro" and mailed in the card with a postal money order for the annual dues. Some weeks later, the ABA returned his money order. With it was a form letter stating that the committee on admissions had not accepted his application. It did not state the reason, but he knew. Blacks were not welcome in the ABA.

"I needed the ABA in those days," Poole said years later. "I needed something to make me feel that I was a lawyer." But the ABA did not want him. Poole joined the National Bar Association.

Around that same time, Cecil Poole met Charlotte Crump. Born in Pittsburg, Texas, she had grown up in St. Paul, Minnesota, where her father, a doctor, had a private practice. Charlotte was raised with all the privileges her parents could give her. She was extremely bright and was only sixteen years old when she graduated from the University of Minnesota, where she studied journalism and political science. For a time, her father refused to let her go out to work because she was still so young. Eventually, however, he relented. Charlotte Crump got a job with the *Pittsburgh Courier*. Starting as a reporter, she quickly moved up to assistant editor.

Charlotte and Cecil were introduced by mutual friends who thought they might make a good couple. They looked as if they belonged together. Charlotte was a beautiful young woman, smart and articulate. Cecil was six feet tall, sported a thin mustache, and was an impeccable dresser. Both were ambitious. The only thing they did not share was a similar background. While Cecil had been raised in a middle-class environment, Charlotte's upbringing had been upper middle class.

Cecil and Charlotte soon fell in love. But both were busy beginning their careers. Not long afterward, Charlotte took a position as editor of a new magazine published out of Philadelphia. There she met Marion Stubbs Thomas and other public-spirited women and joined their efforts to establish a new organization for children. Called Jack & Jill, its mission was to help preserve families and guide children, especially to encourage them to stay in school. It was later incorporated in 1947 as Jack & Jill of America and divided into seven regions across the United States.

The magazine that Charlotte Crump edited couldn't attract enough paid advertising and had trouble selling subscriptions. When it ceased publication, she accepted a position as director of information for the NAACP and moved to New York City, where the organization had its headquarters. By this time, Thurgood Marshall, whom Cecil Poole had met while in college, was special counsel to the NAACP. Charlotte worked closely with Marshall to publicize the organization's activities.

Meanwhile, Poole got his chance to become part of "the New Deal Washington scene." He got a job as an attorney with the National Labor Relations Board. The NLRB investigated charges of unfair labor practices by employers, such as interfering with the formation of labor unions or refusing to bargain with unions. Although Poole's experience with labor unions was confined to knowing a labor organizer back in Pittsburgh when he was young, he knew how to read the law. His job was to study the laws Congress had made concerning labor and labor relations and to advise the members of the board on cases that came before it.

Soon Charlotte joined Poole in Washington, D. C. She took a job as an information specialist with the federal Office of War Information, but she had barely settled in when Poole had to leave Washington. On December 7, 1941, Japanese war planes, launched from carriers at sea, bombed the United States naval fleet at Pearl Harbor, Hawaii, sinking not only U.S. ships but the hopes of millions of Americans that somehow the nation could avoid war. A total of nineteen ships were lost, and more than 2,400 American service personnel and civilians were killed. Moments after receiving the report of the Pearl Harbor bombing, President Franklin D. Roosevelt decided that the United States could no longer stay out of World War II. He sent a memo asking Congress to declare war, and at 12:30 p.m. on December 8, he addressed a joint session of Congress and the nation via radio broadcast. He began, "Yesterday, December 7, 1941, a day that will live in infamy . . . ," and ended by asking Congress to declare war on the Japanese Empire. Soon afterward, the United States also declared war on Germany. The nation was now at war on two fronts, Europe and the Pacific, and all able-bodied men were needed to fight. Cecil Poole was among them. He had barely settled into his government job when a new challenge presented itself to him. Poole was drafted into the United States Army.

Sergeant Cecil F. Poole, about 1942

CHAPTER 4

IN THE SEGREGATED ARMY

THE UNITED STATES HAD USED THE DRAFT, OR CONSCRIPTION into the military, as far back as 1863, during the Civil War. In 1940, with war raging in Europe, the federal government introduced a peacetime draft for the first time. Although America was still officially neutral, the government was doing all it could to prepare for eventual participation. This included training men to fight in the various branches of the military. The Selective Training and Service Act (the official term for the military draft) provided for up to 900,000 men to be in training at any one time and to do limited service (first a year, then eighteen months). After the United States declared war on Germany and Japan, a new selective service act required all men ages 18 to 65 to register with the government. The act also declared all men from the age of 18 to 45 eligible for service. They were to serve until six months after the war ended.

Before Cecil Poole reported for duty in the army, he married Charlotte in a small church wedding in Pittsburgh. Their daughter Patti cherishes one of several photographs that appeared in the *Pittsburgh Courier*. The couple is shown leaving the church, and both have surprised looks on their faces. Without the knowledge of Cecil or Charlotte, the *Courier* had arranged for a group of children to be on hand to greet them as they left the building. There wasn't time for a honeymoon. Poole had to report for military duty almost immediately.

Poole's draft notice ordered him to join the North Atlantic Wing of the Air Transport Command, based at Grenier Field in Manchester, New Hampshire. Its mission was to ship airplanes and supplies to England. Huge cargo planes were loaded with some supplies in Omaha, Nebraska, then flown to Grenier Field. There, additional supplies were on-loaded. They had to be precisely packed because balancing the plane's fuel and cargo weight was very important for the long flight over the Atlantic Ocean.

In those days, blacks in the armed forces served in segregated units and were assigned to hard manual labor or menial jobs, such as building fortifications, moving supplies, or waiting tables in the officers' mess hall. The white military hierarchy did not believe blacks had the courage or the intelligence to serve in combat roles. Accordingly, Poole was assigned to an all-black squadron that did manual labor. His commanding officer quickly recognized his leadership abilities, and within a few short months, Private Cecil Poole was promoted to staff sergeant. He had charge of a crew that loaded the cargo planes bound for England.

Pure chance catapulted Sergeant Cecil Poole into military law. A white soldier on the base who faced a court-martial rejected the defense attorney selected for him, forcing the base command to look for another attorney. In those days before computers, the system for organizing men by education and experience used paper forms that were coded with holes punched in certain places. To find all the people on the base with legal experience, a long metal needle was inserted into a particular hole in a stack of forms. All the forms that came up on the needle were possible matches for the kind of experience needed. In that way, Poole's legal credentials came to the attention of the base command.

The forms of several men on the base had come up on the needle. All the others were white. But the defendant, a big, powerful man who was also white, chose Poole to serve as his defense attorney.

When Poole's commanding officer told him the base commandant wanted to see him up at headquarters, Poole's first response was, 'What have I done?' He was relieved but also wary when he learned he had been selected to be defense counsel in the military. It was highly unusual for a man unfamiliar with the military justice system to serve as defense counsel at a general court-martial.

The military justice system is similar to the civilian criminal justice system, but there are differences. Military attorneys go through several months of formal training to learn the military justice system and the court-martial process. They are also usually on personal terms with the military judge and familiar with how he runs a court-martial. Needless to say, Poole, a black attorney in the segregated army, had none of this background.

Poole met and interviewed his client, a man who had been in trouble before. He studied the accusations his client's captain had made against him and concluded that the army had a solid case. He also studied the military legal system and prepared to defend his client in a general court-martial, the most serious court-martial. It would be presided over by a judge—a senior military attorney who was either a general or an admiral. There would be at least five members of the court (they were not called a jury). There would be a prosecuting counsel and a defense counsel. Since both would be members of the military, they would observe the rules of military courtesy. Poole would not have the opportunity to jump up and cry, "I object, Your Honor!"

At the court-martial, Poole did respectfully raise several objections when he believed they were in order. In each case, the judge sustained them. For example, when the captain who had made the complaint testified and Poole felt he wasn't giving responsive answers, the judge directed the captain to do so.

As Poole had expected, his client was convicted and sentenced to three years in jail, followed by a dishonorable discharge. Nevertheless, the sentence could have been much harsher.

"They had said he was looking at fifteen [years in jail]," Poole remembered. "He asked me to come down to the stockade shortly after that. He said, 'I'm never going to forget this. Look, I'll do that time, don't worry about me, I'll do that time. But boy, you should have seen that major's face when they sustained your objections.'"

Word got around the base that Poole was a good defense counsel, and he was asked to work on several other cases. None of them reached the court-martial stage. Instead, Poole advised his clients that they could not possibly win in a military trial. He often arranged for his clients to plead guilty to lesser charges.

Poole's obvious intelligence and ability soon led him to Officer Candidate School. It was called Air Force Administrative School to distinguish it from pilot training. When Poole entered the school, it had just been relocated from a base near San Antonio, Texas, to Maxwell Field, near Montgomery, Alabama.

That Deep South city was as segregated as Poole's birth city of Birmingham, Alabama. Poole called it a "bastion of ignorance." At Maxwell Field, all the men, white and black, referred to each other as Mister. Off the base, in Montgomery, no white man would have called a black man Mister. In fact, in the Montgomery area, as elsewhere in the Deep South, black men were called by their first names. Elderly black men might be called Uncle; anyone younger was often called Boy.

Maxwell Field was split in two by the long runways required by the B-29 bomber, the largest bomber in the world at that time. The administrative offices, the barracks, the cadet barracks, and the swimming pool and recreation facilities were on one side of the runways. On the other side was a black labor battalion. This battalion had its own swimming pool, its own barracks, it own mess hall, and its own theater. There was no reason for the blacks to cross over to the other side of the runways unless they were on official assignment.

At first, Cecil Poole's experience on the base was different from that of the vast majority of other blacks there. Because he was assigned to Officer Candidate School, Poole was on the "white side." He was the only black person in his class and one of only three in the school. The other two were a year or so ahead of him. Soon all three were subjected to the humiliation of southern race laws.

One morning, after Poole had been at the base for two or three weeks, his class was told they were going to aquatics, by which was meant swimming lessons. They were in the swimming pool on the white side of the base when a jeep drove up and a young lieutenant got out and spoke to the aquatics instructor. The instructor, using the military practice of calling everyone Mister, called out, "Mr. Poole, the lieutenant wants to talk to you."

The lieutenant drove Poole to the commandant's headquarters. There Poole was surprised to see the other two blacks from OCS. All three were informed that in the future they were to have their aquatics training across the field at the black labor battalion's swimming pool. Despite feeling insulted and humiliated, the two upperclassmen were prepared to obey the commandant's order. Poole was not and he said so.

"What do you mean you won't obey that order?" the commandant said. "This is an order, and when you get an order in the military, you obey an order." Poole responded, "I think, sir, that is so, unless the order is so offensive that it can't be a valid order."

"Well, this is an order," said the commandant, "and if you disobey that order, you will be court-martialed, do you understand that? We'll put a court-martial together before you can turn around."

Poole asked for the opportunity to select his own counsel and named two people. One of them was Thurgood Marshall. The base commander was not impressed, for he had never heard of Marshall, but most black Americans had. By this time, Marshall was chief counsel for the NAACP. Using the law to benefit blacks had become the NAACP's primary focus, and as chief counsel, based at the organization's headquarters in New York City, Marshall was probably the most important black attorney in the country.

Although he did not know who Thurgood Marshall was, the base commander understood that Poole was ready to seek the advice of a lawyer. He didn't especially want that, so he tried another approach. He suggested that Poole resign from Officer Candidate School if he was unwilling to obey orders. Poole replied to that suggestion, "Sir, if I did that, I could never prove that I would otherwise have been able to finish this training." Realizing that Poole was not going to back down, the commandant consulted with some other officers, then ordered Poole to return to his quarters. The incident was never mentioned again. But never again did Poole and the other two black cadets take part in aquatics training.

Not long after this incident, an officer informed Poole that if he ever wished to visit the other side of the runways (the side for blacks), all he had to do was call the motor pool and someone would drive him over. He told a couple of his classmates, and they began to laugh, "Hey, hey, we've got us a car!" Instead of going to the black enlisted men's side of the base, Poole and his friends went for rides in the motor pool car.

Poole was proud when he received his commission as an officer. He was in the top five in his class in academics. He was also in the top five in athletics. As a former high school track team member, he was a great runner. He later joked, "I could outrun almost everybody in the class, so I got along fine."

Receiving his commission also meant that Poole would be leaving Maxwell Field and its rigid segregation. Although his first assignment as an officer was also in Alabama, it was a very different kind of military base. Tuskegee Air Force Base was located on the grounds of the all-black Tuskegee Institute. The base existed for the specific purpose of training black pilots.

Before reporting for their new assignments, all the commissioned officers were granted a ten-day furlough. Poole decided to spend it with relatives in his birth city of Birmingham, Alabama. But the commission award ceremony was delayed for two days, and when he tried to board a bus to Birmingham, he found there was no more room. Remembering the one advantage he had enjoyed at segregated Maxwell Field, he called the base motor pool and ordered an army jeep to take him to Birmingham. Years later, he still chuckled when he told the story of how he left Maxwell Field for the last time.

Tuskegee Air Force Base was the headquarters of the 99th Fighter Squadron, the first group of black pilots and support troops to be selected for combat training by the United States military. The NAACP and other civil rights organizations had pushed for the training of black pilots as the nation mobilized for war back in the late 1930s. In 1940, President Roosevelt directed the War Department to create a black flying unit, and Tuskegee Army Airfield was established for this purpose. The training program there became known as the "Tuskegee Experiment" because United States Army officials doubted that blacks were capable of combat flying.

Cecil Poole was assigned to the position of assistant trial judge advocate with the 332nd Fighter Group, which consisted of three fighter squadrons, the 100th, 301st, and 302nd. But he did not have many trials to deal with. The black aviation cadets were very serious and intent on proving their worth and not inclined to make trouble. He spent much of his time accompanying cadets on their training flights. The planes they flew at the time were B-17 biplanes. The Tuskegee airstrip was not equipped for night flights, so the cadets from Tuskegee had to go to Maxwell Field in Montgomery to do their flying after dark.

The military worried about sending the 99th Fighter Squadron into combat. The army "brass," as the highest officials were called, feared that the first all-black unit would negatively affect the morale of the white pilots and troops. The War Department kept looking for a place in the world to send them where they wouldn't be resented.

Finally, in April 1943, twenty-three pilots, engineers, grounds-crewmen, and messmen of the 99th were posted to North Africa. This was an important battleground, for both the German Nazis and their Italian Fascist allies were trying to gain control there. The British and Americans were determined that they would not. Members of the 99th flew strafing missions and also flew escort for other bombers. They participated in the invasion of Sicily, where two pilots were shot down in the fighting. Although the area commander commended the 99th, the leader of another fighter group wrote that the 99th was not sufficiently disciplined in the air and did not operate well enough as a team.

American public opinion was equally divided about the black pilots. Although more and more units were being trained back at Tuskegee, U.S. military authorities were still slow to send them into combat. Eventually, the 332nd Fighter Group joined the 99th Pursuit Squadron in Italy, arriving just days after the most important victories in the short history of the 99th. By the time Germany surrendered on May 8, 1945, the black pilots—not to mention black ground combat forces—had proven both their skill and their bravery. With the surrender of Japan on August 14, 1945, World War II was over.

Poole never left the United States. Each time he thought he would be sent overseas, something happened to delay his orders to ship out. He was preparing to go to the Pacific front when the United States dropped atomic bombs on the cities of Hiroshima and Nagasaki in Japan, and Japan surrendered.

Poole could have continued serving in the army after the war was over. But he believed the United States military had a long way to go before it was truly desegregated, and he wasn't interested in helping that process along. He was eager to get back to civilian life and to the career that the war had interrupted. He could hardly wait to be a civilian trial attorney. Honorably discharged, Poole, like most other World War II veterans, continued to wear his uniform for some time, proud to show that he had served his country.

Proud of having served his country, Poole still wore his uniform when he and Charlotte decided to move to California.

CHAPTER 5

CALIFORNIA, HERE THEY COME!

STILL WEARING HIS UNIFORM WHEN HE APPEARED IN PUBLIC, Cecil Poole rejoined Charlotte in Washington, D.C. She was still working in the Office of War Information, but Poole needed a job. Through a mutual friend, he and Charlotte met Ben C. Duniway, the West Coast regional director of the Office of Price Administration(OPA). The OPA had been established during the war to create and enforce guidelines for the cost of everything from butter to apartment rents.

In their frequent letters to each other during the war, Cecil and Charlotte Poole talked about what they would do when peace was restored. Both wanted to live in California. When they met Duniway, they mentioned their goal, and the OPA executive said to look him up when they got out there. Before they made their big move, Charlotte returned to her family's home in St. Paul, Minnesota, for a medical operation. In her absence, Poole saw to the shipping of their few belongings from Washington, D.C., to friends in Oakland, California. Then he drove to St. Paul. Once Charlotte had recovered from her surgery, the couple set off on their big adventure, driving across the country to San Francisco.

It was no pleasure trip. The major interstate highways had not yet been built, and driving was often slow. But the chief difficulty for the Pooles as they made their way across the country was finding places to stay. "They hit a lot of places where they couldn't rent a room," said their daughter Patti. "I think it was in Colorado where every place they tried had no vacancies. But then they met a bellhop. He said, 'I have this friend who has a room.' And it was kind of like a basement room. My dad said that the room had a chamber pot, and my mother said, 'What is *that* for?'"

When they finally arrived in San Francisco, they were surprised by the climate. Poole recalled, "This was January and it was cold as hell in San Francisco, and I had always thought it was going to be dancing girls and palm trees and sandy beaches. . . . Boy, was it cold. I was so disappointed."

There were other ways in which San Francisco was not especially warm, but these had nothing to do with climate. The city's white inhabitants were unprepared for the influx of blacks who came between 1940 and 1950 looking for war jobs, many of them at the navy shipyard at Hunters Point. The black population of the city grew tenfold during that decade, coming up against considerable discrimination. The city's municipal railway made black people sit in designated cars or sections of cars. Labor unions refused to accept black members. Many white landlords would not rent to black people. White San Franciscans appeared to believe that blacks would just go away if they were not welcomed.

Thomas C. Fleming was then the young owner-editor of *The Reporter*, a small black weekly newspaper in San Francisco. He recalls attending a press conference when Roger Lapham was mayor of the city (1944–48). After the conference, Lapham approached him and asked, "Mr. Fleming, how long do you think these colored people are going to be here?" According to Fleming, "I looked him in the eye and said, 'Mr. Mayor, do you know how permanent the Golden Gate [Bridge] is?' He said yes. I said, 'Well, the black population is just as permanent. They're here to stay, and the city fathers may as well make up their minds to find housing and employment for them, because they're not going back down South.' He turned red in the face. That was the only exchange of words I ever had with him."

When the Pooles arrived in San Francisco, the issue of restrictive covenants was often in the news. Restrictive covenants dated back to the 1870s, when many Asians were brought in to work on the railroads. Fearful that those foreigners might want to live near them, white Californians began to enter into agreements not to rent or sell to non-whites. Under those agreements, the Asian immigrants— and any other people considered undesirable—could occupy residences only as servants. They could not buy property. By the twentieth century, restrictive covenants were also used to keep out blacks, Mexicans, and Jews. Most Mexicans were too poor and politically powerless to fight against covenants. But well-to-do blacks and Jews were mounting increasingly strong attacks.

In Los Angeles, home of the Hollywood entertainment industry, a growing number of blacks were able to afford homes in expensive neighborhoods. But those neighborhoods all had restrictive covenants. Black musician Benny Carter and black singer June Richmond brought suit against the covenants. So did a number of

Jews. The issue of restrictive covenants went all the way to the United States Supreme Court. In early 1948, the court ruled in the case of *Shelley v. Kraemer* that federal and state courts could not enforce restrictive covenants. While the court did not actually declare the covenants illegal, most people thought it had. Blacks and Jews saw the decision as a major victory. The campaign against the covenants gained momentum.

That same year, musician and actor Nat "King" Cole quietly bought a home in the exclusive Hancock Park section of Los Angeles. Nearly one hundred residents of the area sued Cole and his wife to prevent them from moving in. The NAACP, the local chapter of the Congress of Industrial Organizations (CIO), a group of labor unions, the American Civil Liberties Union (ACLU), and the Anti-Defamation League of B'nai B'rith came to Cole's defense. Eventually, Cole and his wife moved into their home. The following year, black actress and singer Lena Horne and her white Jewish husband Lennie Hayton suffered similar trouble when they bought a home in the Nichols Canyon area of Los Angeles.

Cecil and Charlotte Poole were just starting out in California, and they didn't have the money to live in a middle-class neighborhood, so restrictive covenants were not a problem they experienced at first hand. Their friends in Oakland found them a place to stay at 5300 Manila Avenue in a black residential area near the border of the city of Berkeley. As much as possible, they avoided situations that would insult their dignity.

Once they had settled in, Cecil Poole contacted Ben C. Duniway about a job with the West Coast Office of Price Administration. He was hired as a research attorney for the region. With the war over, price controls were being lifted, and personnel were either resigning or being laid off. It was not long before Poole became the chief of the West Coast Regional Briefing and Appellate Office. He had charge of appellate litigation, cases in which decisions by the OPA were appealed. Most of his work centered on cases in Oregon. Many judges in that state had refused to enforce price controls, and it was his job to pursue the matter in the Oregon Supreme Court.

In the meantime, Poole studied for the California bar exam. He had been out of law school since 1939, and California law differed in many respects from Pennsylvania law. Still, he passed on his first try. Now he could practice in that state and represent clients in court.

Once he was notified that he had passed the bar, Poole attempted to resign from the Office of Price Administration. The OPA was practically shut down by then, but since there were a few cases remaining, he was asked to see them to conclusion. He finished out those cases in early 1948.

This was not full-time work, so Poole had time to investigate other opportunities and eventually went into private practice, renting an office on Sutter Street. Charlotte Poole was her husband's secretary. Poole had a general practice, which means he took various kinds of cases and didn't specialize in any particular type. Poole's diary from that time shows that much of his work was in wills and estates.

One of Poole's bigger cases was a discrimination suit filed against a San Francisco hotel. A Los Angeles-based theatrical group was traveling with a show called "Deep Are the Roots" that had an interracial cast. They had a booking in San Francisco and had made advance reservations at a Geary Street hotel. When they arrived, they were told there was a mistake and the hotel had no rooms. The group contacted Poole, who filed a lawsuit against the hotel. To make sure the hotel management knew he was serious, he sued for $10,000, even though he was quite sure he would never get that amount. The hotel soon gave in and offered to settle the case out of court. The troupe did not want to settle, but Poole persuaded them that it was the best course. The hotel paid his five-hundred-dollar attorney's fee and court costs. Poole also insisted that the hotel post a written declaration that it would not discriminate against any guests on account of race. That, he told his clients, was worth more than $10,000 in the long run. Eventually, other hotels in the city also stopped their discriminatory practices.

As educated black professionals, Cecil and Charlotte Poole were in a small group in the San Francisco area. They soon knew everyone in the group and became active in civic and political causes. They joined the local black Democratic political organization and the San Francisco branch of the NAACP. Poole later became president of the chapter and, once his term as president was over, a director.

Pursuing his career in law, Poole listed himself with the various state courts and got some work as a court-appointed attorney defending accused criminals who could not afford to hire a lawyer of their own. In one such case, he found himself opposite Edmund G. "Pat" Brown, then district attorney for San Francisco. Poole's efforts to bring the matter to conclusion impressed Brown, who later offered Poole a job in the district attorney's office. Poole happily accepted.

Honoree and attendees at testimonial dinner given for Cecil Poole, assistant district attorney of San Francisco, March 16, 1954. Standing, left to right: George O'Leary, Al Birdsall, Emil Dutil, George Hoover, Mike Doherty, Mel Jorgensen, George Heeg, Jules Zimmerlin, Marion Overstreet, Charles Sutton. Seated, left to right: Max Girard, Ed O'Haire, Capt. James English, Cecil Poole, Lt. Martin Lee, Tom Cahill, and Glenn Gravatt.

CHAPTER 6

ASSISTANT DISTRICT ATTORNEY

A DISTRICT ATTORNEY IS THE CHIEF PROSECUTING OFFICER of a judicial district. In a large city like San Francisco—which is a district in itself—the district attorney employs many assistant district attorneys. As the newest assistant, Cecil Poole got the lowest job. Assigned to the municipal court complaints desk, he attended to minor complaints brought by ordinary citizens—complaints about quality-of-life issues, like noisy dogs. Although these complaints might be minor in the grand scheme of things, they were major to the people making them. Irate people would often announce, "I am a taxpayer," as if that gave them the right not to be bothered by a clanging trash truck. Poole's sense of humor would sometimes get the better of him and he would say, "Oh, do you have your tax receipt with you?"

It wasn't just ordinary citizens who would come to Poole's desk with complaints. San Francisco police officers brought their arrests to him also. Poole was shocked when officers would announce to him, "We busted four niggers tonight." He couldn't believe his ears. Not only did they use that racial epithet, they used it in his presence. To the chief inspector of the police department, to the chief assistant district attorney, and to the district attorney himself, Poole announced that he would throw into the wastebasket the complaint of any officer who used that kind of language. Over time, he made his point. Occasionally, an officer would slip, but he would quickly apologize to Poole.

Poole's duties as an assistant district attorney also included attending preliminary hearings. In California there are two ways of deciding whether enough evidence exists to bind an arrested person over for trial. Prosecution may be initiated by either a judicial preliminary hearing or a criminal grand jury indictment. A judicial preliminary hearing is public. It allows the defense attorney to understand the charges and the evidence against the defendant. It also allows the prosecuting attorney—usually an assistant D.A.—to establish the state's case against the defendant.

A case that does not go through a preliminary hearing is heard by a grand jury. Composed of ordinary citizens, this panel hears the evidence and decides if it is sufficient to indict the person charged with a crime. Grand jury proceedings are closed to the general public. Poole's duties also included reading the transcripts, usually word-for-word records, of grand jury hearings.

From time to time, Poole would receive an invitation in the mail to join the American Bar Association. Remembering his earlier rejection, he would throw it away. But the ABA was persistent. The organization's power and influence depended on a large membership, and it was always actively recruiting new members. Not long after he was hired as an assistant district attorney, Poole was visited by two young attorneys representing the ABA. He listened politely as they explained the benefits of membership to him. Then he told them about his experience as a new lawyer. They were shocked and dismayed that he had been denied membership because of his race. They told him that he could help break down the racial barriers in the ABA. But Poole was not interested in helping the ABA.

Poole had been on the job as assistant district attorney only a few weeks when one of his superiors assigned him to read more transcripts of grand jury hearings and spend less time at the complaints desk. Such a quick promotion was unusual and caused some grumbling among others on the complaints desk. But Poole still had plenty of low-level assignments, including the prosecution of minor cases.

One so-called minor case threatened to become major. Like many other municipal court cases, it involved a traffic ticket. This particular ticket, however, had been handed to a prominent, black San Francisco pediatrician, Dr. Carlton Goodlett, who was determined to fight the citation.

Born in a small town in southern Florida, Goodlett considered California to be "the last frontier" in race relations, and he dedicated himself to fighting racism wherever and whenever he found it. In the late 1940s, he and Dr. Daniel Collins, a local black dentist, purchased and merged two struggling black newspapers and created the San Francisco *Sun-Reporter*. The newspaper gave Goodlett a platform for launching a steady assault on racial discrimination. He and Collins also started the Democratic Party's first black club in San Francisco and were active in the local chapter of the NAACP.

According to Thomas C. Fleming, who served as editor of the *Sun-Reporter*, a police officer on a motorcycle claimed that he had been following Goodlett for a number of blocks and that he had gone through a red light. Goodlett asked, "Why didn't you stop me before now?" The officer asked to see Goodlett's license, looked at it, and began, "Well, Carlton. . . ." Goodlett bristled. "Listen here," he said, "I'm Dr. Goodlett to you, and you're Officer to me." The officer said, "Get out of the car." Goodlett replied, "I'm not getting out of this goddamn car. You tell me why you stopped me." The officer then forced him out of the car, handcuffed him, took him down to the Hall of Justice, and booked him for both the traffic violation and resisting arrest. Thomas Fleming paid Dr. Goodlett's bail, and he was released.

In Poole's opinion, the case never should have gone to trial, for Goodlett admitted going through a red light. However, Poole understood Goodlett's fury over his mistreatment at the hands of the racist police officer, so he attempted to mediate. He asked for a conference with the judge who was trying the case and persuaded the judge that pursuing the case would serve no purpose. The judge agreed to dismiss all charges except the charge of failing to stop at the red light. He levied a fine of five dollars. But Goodlett stood on principal and refused to pay the fine. Poole offered to pay it for him. On hearing of Poole's offer, the judge suspended the fine.

Goodlett, a self-described "champion of the people," had a long and distinguished career in San Francisco. In 1963, he built a combination medical and newspaper office on Turk Street near Fillmore that became a center for civil rights work in the city. After Goodlett died in 1997, Mayor Willie Brown designated the address of the newly refurbished City Hall as Dr. Carlton B. Goodlett Place.

Not long after that case—and perhaps in part because of it—District Attorney Edmund Brown invited Poole to apply for a promotion. Brown warned, however, that there might be some sensitive cases he would not assign to Poole—instances in which a black person accused a white person of a crime, or vice versa. Brown was concerned that some members of the predominantly white San Francisco police force might tamper with evidence or otherwise attempt to undermine such cases if a black assistant D.A. were involved. Poole was upset by Brown's implications, but he reserved his opinion and said he would have to think about it. At home he discussed the issue with Charlotte. They agreed that Poole would accept no restrictions because of his race. "If that's the way the office is to be run," he told Brown, "I think it would be a grave mistake to have me in it. You're the district attorney. You have to make your own decisions on who's going to do what in your office, and I can appreciate that. . . . But I don't think I want to come to work for you under these conditions."

Brown apologized and admitted he was embarrassed that he had even raised the issue. He assured Poole that there would be no assignment of cases based on race. Poole moved to the main office of the San Francisco district attorney. It was 1949, and he was thirty-five years old.

By this time, Edmund Brown had decided to run for the office of attorney general of the state of California. In November of the following year, he won election to that office. Mayor Elmer Robinson appointed Brown's top assistant, Thomas Lynch, to succeed him. Brown invited Poole to go with him to the state attorney's office, but Poole chose to remain with the San Francisco D.A.'s office. Although the pay in the state attorney general's office was higher, accepting Brown's offer would mean moving to the state capital, Sacramento. The Pooles liked living in San Francisco. Besides, while working with the San Francisco D.A., Poole was able to take on a few private clients, and he decided that was enough to make up the difference in pay.

Thomas Lynch reorganized the San Francisco D.A.'s office and promoted Poole to the position of chief of the Superior Court division staff. The superior court is a trial court; as chief, Poole had direction over all the trial lawyers. Some of those trial lawyers refused to work under a black attorney and left the D.A.'s office, but most remained.

As a black man in America, Poole encountered racism of one sort or another almost on a daily basis, in and out of the workplace. He was not immune even when he was in court, prosecuting a case. One judge, an older woman who substituted for vacationing superior court judges, refused to recognize Poole's position, asking, "Young man, do you have counsel?" On another occasion, Poole recommended that a substantial bail be set for police officers under indictment. The same judge said, "Young man, I am surprised at you. You, of all people, ought to know the hardship of having a high bail." Realizing that she must consider most blacks criminals, Poole assured the judge that being handed a traffic ticket was his only criminal experience.

Poole liked trying cases in court himself. He estimated that, in the ten years he served as chief of the Superior Court Division staff, he personally tried about 115 cases. Reading trial transcripts when he first arrived in the district attorney's office proved excellent preparation for courtroom work. He understood the importance of those pages of typed testimony. When he was trying a case in court, he made sure to get that day's testimony the same evening. After sitting up until the early hours of the morning carefully reading the transcript and making notes, he would walk back into the court in full command of the previous day's proceedings.

Poole tried so many cases that in later years only a few stood out in his mind. One of the most poignant was a case of rape. The victim was a part-white, part-Native American girl born in Arizona, who had been adopted as a child by a white couple. Later, the family had moved to San Francisco. While at a party in the city, the young woman was kidnapped and raped by three men, who then drove her to her home. Her parents called an ambulance and reported the crime to the police. Others at the party had seen the young woman being driven away in the car by her abductors and had been able to identify the men. Poole took the case, which appeared to be fairly cut-and-dried. He had witnesses and the girl's own testimony, as well as physical evidence. But the outcome of a jury trial can never be certain. Private citizens can be easily swayed, and some will act out of prejudices they don't even know they have. Poole always believed that it was not the evidence but racial prejudice that made the difference in that case.

The defendants' attorneys argued that the young woman was not forced to have sex with the men, but had gone willingly with them. Every day in court, two priests and two nuns attended, sitting close to the front and clearly in attendance to support the defendants and their families. One priest testified to the good character of the young men. The girl did not attend church regularly, even though her adoptive parents were missionaries.

After a lengthy deliberation, the jury found the young men not guilty. Poole was astonished and angry. He believed that the church had been exploited—used to protect guilty men who did not deserve its help. He said as much to members of the jury with whom he later spoke. Forty-odd years later, that case still bothered him. He always believed that the jury had wrongly blamed the victim.

In another memorable case, the good-character testimony by two priests failed to help a defendant. This was a man accused of murdering his estranged wife. After she left him, she took a lover and gave birth to a child. Then the second man, a sailor, was killed. The husband was willing to take his wife back, but he did not want a baby that was not his. She refused to abandon her baby. In what would be called "stalking" today, the husband followed her everywhere she went, called her on the telephone, lurked about her residence in Fresno, California. She was so afraid of him that she fled to San Francisco. Since her parents were Russian, she sought help from the Russian consulate there and was given refuge. Her husband found out where she was staying and tried to see her, but he was denied entry. He waited until her birthday and hired a man to pose as a singing messenger. When the woman appeared at the door to receive her birthday message, her husband stepped from the shadows and shot her to death.

Poole, the chief prosecutor on the case, was willing to charge the defendant with second-degree murder. But the defense attorney, a well-known lawyer in San Francisco named Leo Sullivan, insisted that the charge be reduced to assault with a deadly weapon. In response, Poole upped the charge to first-degree murder. The defendant's family was in court every day to support him, and so were two family priests. But this time the jury was not swayed by their presence. They returned a verdict of guilty of murder in the first degree. The sentence for this charge was life imprisonment.

Poole had some sympathy for the man. He did not feel that a life term would serve justice and shared his feelings with the judge, who reduced the charge to second-degree murder. This charge carried a prison sentence, but not life imprisonment. The man served eight or nine years in jail and, while there, wrote often to both Poole and the judge. He also started writing screenplays while in prison and managed to sell one of them. On his release from prison on parole, he bought a share of a trucking business and never had further trouble with the law. Poole always believed he had made a difference in the man's life and was proud of it. Even though his job was to prosecute criminals, he did not believe that all criminals were equally bad.

Two daughters were born to Cecil and Charlotte Poole during his service with the San Francisco D.A.'s office: Gayle Alexandra in 1947 and Patricia Mary five years later. Gayle showed early artistic talent, and Patti was reading by the age of three.

"By the time I was old enough to be aware of anything, I knew that my dad was special," Patti Poole recalls. "I just grew up with it; it was part of my life. I mean, when Dad was in the D.A.'s office, there was a TV show called *San Francisco Beat*. They often used his office for background shots. It was near Chinatown, and it had these beautiful arched windows. Dad used to bring the actors and crew home all the time. I probably met many of the most important movers and shakers in San Francisco over the years, but they were just nice people to me, just friends of my parents."

By the time Patti entered kindergarten, the Pooles were looking for a larger house. They were comfortable financially and could afford it. But they ran up against the same problem that had beset Nat "King" Cole and his wife and other successful blacks in

California. The areas with the big houses were white areas. Blacks were not welcome.

Realtors were polite and helpful in telephone conversations, nervous and apologetic when they met the Pooles and saw they were black. A realtor was showing them a house one day when he suddenly announced, "We've got to get out of here. They're bringing some people in." Poole asked why they had to leave. The realtor answered, "I'm not supposed to do this." It suddenly dawned on Poole that the realtor expected them, a black couple, to escape out the back door before a white couple came through the front door and saw them. He said, "Come on, Charlotte, let's go. We're going out the front door the way we came in." To the realtor, he said, "By the way, good-bye."

Eventually, after enduring several insulting incidents, the Pooles found in the residential neighborhood of Ingleside Terrace a large house whose owners were willing to sell to a black family. The house had been built in 1910, on a corner lot in what was then the first housing development west of the Twin Peaks. The fourteen-room, two-story house was built entirely of redwood, complete with burl-paneled walls, parquet floors, leaded glass windows, and a full basement.

Patti remembers being welcomed by the neighborhood children, one of whom became her best friend. Some adults, however, were not so pleased to see the Pooles. Patti recalled her father explaining later that some of the neighbors didn't believe a four-member black family could afford a house that size and feared that an entire clan might move in—a big, extended family who would even occupy the garage. The Pooles, of course, planned for their cars to occupy the garage, and that was all.

"I was still going to my old kindergarten, which was close to where we used to live," says Patti. "My Dad would drive me there in the morning before he went to work. The garage [of the new house] was separate from the house, and I used to have this game with my father—a race to see who could reach the garage first. He'd start off in the family room and go out the back door and through the back yard. I would go out the front door and cut across the side lawn. "Well, one morning I ran smack into a cross. There was a wooden cross on our front lawn, and it was burning. I ran to find my dad and took him to see the burnt cross.

"My dad said something like, 'It's just an angel who lost his way.' Then he quickly took me back into the house. My mother wouldn't let me go to school that day. I didn't know why at the time."

Four-year-old Patti Poole was too young to understand that someone had burned a cross on the Pooles' front lawn to try to frighten them into leaving the neighborhood, a tactic the Ku Klux Klan often used. While her mother kept her busy inside the house, her father called the police. Patti later learned that he did not disturb the cross until the police arrived to inspect the area for evidence. Only after the investigation was finished did he take the cross down.

That was the only outright threat the Pooles received in their new neighborhood, and it was not enough to make Cecil and Charlotte Poole consider leaving. In fact, it made them even more determined to stay. Although they endured insults as the only black people in the area, they did not dwell on them.

Says Judge Charles Renfrew, who later came to know Poole well, "Cecil was someone who would never forget things. But he wasn't a person who kept a tally of injustices and wrongs and lashed out. He remembered because they made an impact and they were harmful and they were hurtful, but he went forward. He was somebody who picked himself up and dusted himself off. . . . [H]e was a very positive person who went ahead."

Patti was happy in the house in Ingleside Terrace. She and her best friend Kathy made the basement their playhouse. She remembers some name-calling at school, but no serious problems. The same was not true for her older sister, Gayle. "It was mostly name-calling, but it was harder on her because she was the first black kid in her class," Patti explained. "By the time she got to high school, there were a lot of black kids. The problem we both had—when she was in high school and I was in junior high school—was with the black kids that were bused in from outside the area. When [the city of San Francisco] started busing to achieve racial integration in the schools, they brought black kids in from a couple of miles away. And a lot of them resented the fact that we lived in that upper-class neighborhood. They'd tell me I was stuck up because my best friend was white. I had black friends, too, but they didn't see that. They just saw that my best friend was white.

"Every once in a while, something would happen," Patti continued. "Like in gym, I'd bend down to tie my shoelace, and someone might kick me.

"Gayle had a lot of problems like that at Lincoln High School, and she was very disturbed by it. I went to a different high school, Lowell High, which was a 'college prep' school and you had to have a certain grade point average to get in. The ethnic makeup and the overall attitude were a lot different there."

Both Cecil and Charlotte Poole ached for their daughters when the girls suffered racial taunts and problems. One or the other of them would visit a school to lodge a complaint when necessary. But they knew the girls would have to make their own way in a racially charged society. For the most part, they counseled their daughters to believe in and stand up for themselves. They were as good as anyone else, and much was expected of them. But facing racism on an almost daily basis sometimes drained the soul.

Cecil F. Poole, special assistant to Governor Edmund G. "Pat" Brown, about 1960.

CHAPTER 7

THE GOVERNOR'S SPECIAL ASSISTANT

WHILE POOLE WAS COURAGEOUSLY RESISTING RACIAL TERRORISM in his own neighborhood and counseling his daughters to be brave at school, momentous changes were taking place in the United States. They would affect the daily lives of the Poole family as well as Cecil Poole's career.

The changes actually started long before World War II, but the war and its aftermath served to accelerate them. President Franklin D. Roosevelt died in 1945, the year the war ended, and Vice President Harry S. Truman succeeded to the presidency. Among the Roosevelt initiatives that President Truman continued were steps toward racial integration. In December 1946, he set up a President's Commission on Civil Rights. The following June, as the first American president to speak at an NAACP convention, he said, "We must make the federal government a friendly, vigilant defender of the rights and equalities of all Americans. And again, I mean *all* Americans."

Although many southern Democrats left the party because of Truman's actions in the civil rights arena, he narrowly defeated the Republican candidate, Thomas Dewey, winning the presidency in 1948. Four years later, he decided not to run for a second full term. The next president to be elected was a Republican, General Dwight David Eisenhower. The highly decorated World War II hero, who had commanded the Allied forces in Europe, had never been a very political person. Yet he would preside over eight years of tumultuous change in American race relations, change that had begun under Truman.

Although President Eisenhower was not an activist for civil rights as Truman had been, he believed in moderate change. When he appointed a new chief justice of the United States Supreme Court, he chose Earl Warren, the governor of California. Warren, a liberal Republican, would preside over one of the most activist groups of nine justices the Supreme Court had ever known. They would interpret the United States Constitution much differently from their predecessors and would profoundly change American race law.

Under Warren's leadership, the Court decided the landmark case of *Brown v. Board of Education*. The case concerned the constitutionality of segregated education. NAACP lawyers, including Poole's old friend Thurgood Marshall, presented forceful arguments against segregated schools, proving that the school boards in the case spent more money on white schools, that black schools were always more run down and equipped with fewer books and supplies than white schools, and that black children were psychologically hurt by segregation. The most memorable lines were spoken by NAACP attorney James Nabrit, who said, "Our Constitution has no provision across it that all men are equal but that white men are more equal than others."

Marshall, Nabrit, and the other NAACP attorneys, the lawyers who opposed them, and the nine justices of the U.S. Supreme Court all realized that more than segregated education was at issue. The real issue was legal racial separation in all its forms. Laws providing for separation of the races dated back only to 1895. In that year, the Supreme Court had ruled in the case of *Plessy v. Ferguson* that separating the races was constitutional as long as the accommodations for both were equal. That, of course, had never been true. But it was a strong precedent, and the justices serving on the Supreme Court in 1954 were deeply divided about overturning it.

Warren believed the *Brown v. Board of Education* case was clearcut. The Court had to overturn *Plessy v. Ferguson*. He did not see that as such a legally momentous event. After all, over the years many judicial decisions had chipped away at the doctrine of *Plessy*. In fact, the legal underpinnings of "separate but equal" had so eroded that only the fact remained. Even so, Warren understood that overturning *Plessy* would be a watershed social event. It would change American society, and especially American southern society, forever. He was determined that the Court be unanimous in its opinion. On Monday, May 17, 1954, the decision was announced. Chief Justice Warren read, "We conclude, unanimously, that in the field of public education the doctrine of 'separate but equal' has no place. Separate educational facilities are inherently unequal."

Not since the Emancipation Proclamation nearly a century before had American blacks felt such a sense of celebration and hope. The Supreme Court's decision in *Brown v. Board of Education* was, in truth, the death knell of segregation in this country. If segregation was wrong in education, then it was also wrong in housing, jobs, medical care, public institutions, and public transportation. Most blacks realized that there was a long road ahead, but they felt a renewed determination. As Thurgood Marshall said in 1955, "If we stop now, we're lost. They're going to try everything in the book to get out from under. Our job is to stay ahead of them."

On December 1 of that same year, a forty-two-year-old seamstress named Rosa Parks boarded a bus in Montgomery, Alabama, and sat in the front row of the "Colored" section, the last few rows. As the bus continued on its route, more people got on. Having no place to sit, they stood. The bus driver looked back, saw whites standing, and told the blacks sitting in the front row of the "Colored" section, "Let me have those front seats." No one moved. The driver said, "Y'all better make it light on yourselves and let me have those seats." One by one, the people sitting near Parks got up. She remained seated. She didn't see how giving up her seat was going to make her life better. It seemed to her that the more blacks gave in and complied, the worse they were treated by racist whites. Some people think she remained seated because she was tired. But she was no more tired than usual at the end of a workday. She was just tired of giving in.

The bus driver summoned the police, who arrested Parks, took her to the city jail, fingerprinted and booked her. The news spread like wildfire through Montgomery's black community. Parks was an upstanding citizen who had spent years quietly working behind the scenes for black rights, serving as secretary to the local NAACP and other civil rights organizations. Her only crime was being black. On the day of her trial, a huge crowd of blacks gathered outside the courthouse. Catching sight of Parks in a demure dress, hat, and pearls, a girl in the crowd screamed, "Oh, she's so sweet. They've messed with the wrong one now."

Parks was found guilty of violating the city's segregation laws and given a fine and a suspended sentence. Attorneys for the NAACP appealed the sentence, and eventually the case went all the way to the United States Supreme Court. In the meantime, the black citizens of Montgomery launched a bus boycott. For more than a year, they stayed off the city's buses, returning only after the Supreme Court ruling that segregation on Montgomery's buses was unconstitutional. A young Baptist minister in Montgomery named Martin Luther King, Jr., gained national recognition as one of the leaders of the bus boycott. Building on its momentum, King and other southern ministers formed the Southern Christian Leadership Conference (SCLC) to push for equal rights. The SCLC's first major campaign was for voting rights.

Although Poole played no role in those momentous events, he followed them closely. He bought all the magazines and newspapers he could find and read every word of articles that touched on civil rights events. He was gratified that lawyers and judges were at the cutting edge of change. He also felt understandable pride that a Californian, former Governor Earl Warren, was presiding over landmark Supreme Court decisions such as *Brown v. Board of Education.*

It turned out that Warren's elevation to the United States Supreme Court affected Cecil Poole's own career, but it took almost six years to happen. When Warren left the California governor's mansion in Sacramento, the lieutenant governor, Goodwin Knight, completed his term as governor. In the next election, Knight ran for the office and won. Four years later, he left the governorship to try for a U.S. Senate seat, one of two from California. Poole's friend and former boss, California's Attorney General Edmund "Pat" Brown, ran for governor and won.

Governor Brown set about assembling his team, selecting the best people he knew. Among them was Loren Miller, a black attorney and newspaper publisher in Los Angeles. Miller had been active in the fight against restrictive covenants in California in the 1930s and 1940s. Working with a group of law professors at the University of California, Los Angeles, Miller had also fought against other forms of segregation. Some viewed Miller as a radical, so the governor's decision to appoint him to his staff stirred up a hornet's nest. Although Brown was willing to risk controversy, Miller worried about accepting the job offer. Brown turned to Poole for help; but Poole was unsuccessful in persuading Miller to be the governor's clemency and extradition secretary and legal counsel. Finally, Brown offered the job to Poole.

For Poole, working for the dynamic Governor Brown was a great opportunity. After talking it over with Charlotte, he accepted, joining the staff of the same man who had hired him into the San Francisco district attorney's office ten years before, in 1949. Poole would be based in the state capital, Sacramento, just a ninety-minute drive from the Poole home. His family remained in San Francisco, so Poole shared a Sacramento apartment with William Coblentz, who was special counsel to the governor. Recalled Poole, "The landlady made every effort to pretend I wasn't there."

Poole later rented a house in Sacramento so that he and Charlotte and their daughters could spend the summer as a family. During that time, Charlotte found a house to buy so that the family could remain together in the fall. The Pooles leased out their San Francisco home, and by fall they were settled in—a blisteringly hot change from fog-bound San Francisco.

As clemency secretary, Poole had to advise the governor on capital punishment cases. In a clemency case, the governor decides whether a sentence imposed on a convicted criminal is appropriate. If he feels it is too harsh, he can reduce the severity of the punishment. Most clemency cases that reached the governor of California at that time involved criminals sentenced to death. Governor Brown did not believe in the death penalty. Nevertheless, he was sworn to uphold the laws of the state.

Poole helped make literally life-and-death decisions. He read all the arrest records, trial transcripts, and appeal motions. He studied the reports of the prosecuting attorneys, the trial judge, the prison warden, and the prison chaplain. He summarized all this information in his own report to the governor. He also gave the governor his opinion about whether the accused had been treated fairly by the state of California up to the point of sentencing and whether the death sentence was appropriate for the crime.

From the moment the new governor took the oath of office in early January 1960, a major death penalty case confronted him and his clemency secretary. Convicted kidnapper Caryl Chessman was scheduled for execution in two weeks. Chessman was twenty-seven years old and out on parole from Folsom Prison when he was arrested in Los Angeles in 1948. Newspapers called him the "Red-Light Bandit." This nickname described the way the bandit operated. He approached victims parked in lonely spots, flashed a red light similar to the light used by police to make drivers open the car door, and then robbed them. Sometimes the bandit also took his women victims out of the car and to another place, and forced them to have sex with him. In one instance, he took the woman to his own car a few feet away and assaulted her. In another, he drove a mile away and then committed the assault.

Chessman signed a confession after his arrest, but he later recanted, saying that the confession had been coerced, or forced, from him. He insisted that he was not the Red Light Bandit but knew who was, although he never came up with a name.

Chessman refused to hire an attorney. Instead, he insisted on representing himself. At his trial, he infuriated Judge John Fricke, who repeatedly overruled Chessman's objections, although in general he was fair. It was not Judge Fricke's practice to have a daily transcript, except in unusual circumstances. A court reporter was present throughout the trial, and he made shorthand notes. But these notes were not transcribed, or typed up, each day.

Chessman was found guilty of kidnapping with "bodily harm," a crime that carried the death penalty. The jury that convicted Caryl Chessman could have recommended mercy but chose not to do so. Chessman was sentenced to die in the gas chamber at San Quentin Prison.

Chessman's was the most controversial death penalty case of the decade, if not of the century. While the case went through appeal—several times—Chessman wrote four books in his own defense. When Governor Brown and his clemency secretary took office, Chessman had been on death row for more than a decade.

People in favor of capital punishment were clamoring for justice to be done and the death sentence to be carried out. Those who opposed capital punishment were just as determined that Chessman would not die. Even people who might have favored the death penalty in some cases were not so sure about the Chessman case. After all, none of his victims had died. Pleas on his behalf came from around the world and from some very famous people. Eleanor Roosevelt, the widow of the late president Franklin D. Roosevelt and a world-renowned figure in her own right, was among them. So were the cellist Pablo Casals, the evangelist Reverend Billy Graham, and the poet Robert Frost.

Yet another stay of execution gave Poole an opportunity to study the case. He had serious reservations about the conduct of Chessman's trial. He believed that Chessman should not have been allowed to act as his own counsel. He also felt that the lack of a trial transcript was a serious error and made an appeal likely. The court reporter who had taken notes of the testimony had died. Another court reporter had offered to transcribe the late reporter's shorthand notes, but it came out that the second court reporter was related by marriage to the prosecutor, creating a potential conflict of interest.

Years later, Poole recapped the major reasons why the Chessman case was a matter of such concern: "First of all, it was a death case where there had been no death. Second, there was a question of Judge Fricke's partiality. Third, there was the failure to have a transcript. And fourth, there was the fact that although there was no transcript, the prosecutor had the advantage of having some of it. Then there was Caryl Chessman's stout assertion that he was not the Red Light Bandit, but he knew who it was."

Yet Chessman had been convicted of a crime that carried the death penalty. California law was very specific. Kidnapping meant taking a victim "any distance." So Chessman, who had taken one victim to his car twenty-two feet away and had driven a mile with another, was guilty of kidnapping. "Bodily harm" meant any kind of injury to the body, and sexual assault certainly qualified. Poole knew the governor wanted to grant clemency. But he told Brown, "Under the constitution of this state, you are without authority to do it."

A new date for Chessman's execution had been set in early 1960, and as it approached, protesters dressed as monks paraded barefoot around the capitol building. Letters and telegrams poured in. Brown agonized. He decided to declare a sixty-nine-day reprieve so he could call the legislature into special session and ask the legislators to repeal the statute. Poole tried to talk him out of it. "The legislature is not going to repeal capital punishment, and you know it," he said to the governor. But Brown responded, "I would rather lose my office than let this man die. I just can't do it."

Poole was right. The legislature did not repeal capital punishment. No court ordered a stay of execution. Caryl Chessman was scheduled to die on May 2, 1960.

When that execution was about to take place, Poole arranged for an open telephone line between the governor's office and the room next to the gas chamber at San Quentin. In that way, if anything did happen at the last minute, there would be no need to waste time dialing and waiting for a call to go through. As the seconds ticked away, Poole held the telephone to his ear and watched the governor trying to keep busy at his desk. There was utter silence in the room. Outside, demonstrators yelled and screamed, as if the sheer volume of their voices could somehow stop the inevitable.

At the other end of the telephone line, the warden at San Quentin announced that he was handing the phone over to his deputy warden. The warden had to accompany Chessman on the "death walk" to the gas chamber. Nothing could stop the execution now. Brown left his office and did not return that day.

Poole wanted to get out of Sacramento, but he felt he had to stay to answer questions. He sympathized with Brown. He, too, believed the death penalty was wrong, and he was frustrated at not being able to find a way to stop the state killing of Caryl Chessman. In his time as clemency secretary to Governor Brown, some fifteen other executions took place, but none was as disturbing as that of Caryl Chessman. "The futility of that case—the futility," he said many years later, shaking his head.

Poole was not against capital punishment in all cases. A person who kills a child, a person who tortures another person who is helpless—"I close my eyes and turn my back on those [people]. I simply can't stand it. I can't adopt some rational way of accepting this as not being a forfeiture of the right to exist. We don't have a very high order of qualifications in this life, but it's higher than that." But in a case like that of Caryl Chessman, he couldn't see the point. He did not feel that capital punishment served justice in most cases. Rather he felt that it was a way for people to handle a problem they did not know how else to solve. "When we can't handle something, we get rid of it," he once explained. "That's how we face up to the problems that we can't solve. But we've made certain that this particular problem won't happen again."

Compared to death penalty cases, the extradition cases Poole worked on were far greater in number and usually routine. These cases involved approving the return of accused criminals to the states where they allegedly committed crimes. At that time, the office of the California attorney general processed about fourteen hundred extradition cases per year. For example, if a man accused of robbing a bank in Arkansas were arrested in California, the California authorities couldn't simply send him back to Arkansas without a formal legal procedure. Sometimes, extradition meant sending an accused person to another country, such as Mexico.

Usually, the crimes involved in extradition cases were minor, such as car theft or burglary or bad checks. The state attorney general gathered all the paperwork on a case, and Poole would review it and then advise the governor. If the case were straightforward, he would usually advise the governor to sign the extradition order. But there were some cases that were not quite so cut and dried.

One example was cases involving black people accused of crimes in the South. If it seemed to Poole that the fugitive had been convicted primarily because of his race, then he would advise the governor not to extradite. Another example was cases of prison escape where there was evidence that the fugitive faced injury or death if he were returned to the prison.

A case that was quite a tribute to Poole's compassion and resourcefulness involved a white man in Pennsylvania who killed another white man in a fight. He fled to California, where he married, had children, and held steady jobs for twenty years. Then he retired, and somehow news of his retirement party got back to Pennsylvania. The authorities wanted him extradited, but Poole managed to work out a deal. The man returned to Pennsylvania to face a reduced charge of involuntary manslaughter, was given a suspended sentence, and was allowed to return to his family and resume his life in California.

Poole also advised Governor Brown about various bills being considered by the legislature and helped the governor to campaign for laws he wanted passed. Among the efforts he helped to spearhead was racial integration of the California Highway Patrol (CHP). There had never been a black officer on that force, and both Brown and

Poole believed it was high time. The head of the CHP resisted, claiming that he hired patrolmen for their ability, not their color. Poole informed the man that there were blacks with ability. He added that the governor expected other qualified citizens besides whites to have the opportunity to serve in the CHP. Eventually, the head of the CHP relented and hired the first black patrolman. It was one of Poole's more satisfying victories during his two-and-a-half years advising the governor of California. He may not have marched and boycotted and sat in and engaged in other direct-action civil rights demonstrations in the South, but he contributed to the overturning of racial barriers when he could.

Cecil F. Poole is sworn in as United States attorney for the Northern District of California, the first black U.S. attorney in the continental United States, June 1961. With him are his wife, Charlotte, and his daughters Patti and Gayle.

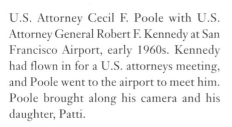

U.S. Attorney Cecil F. Poole with U.S. Attorney General Robert F. Kennedy at San Francisco Airport, early 1960s. Kennedy had flown in for a U.S. attorneys meeting, and Poole went to the airport to meet him. Poole brought along his camera and his daughter, Patti.

CHAPTER 8

CECIL F. POOLE, UNITED STATES ATTORNEY

INTEGRATING THE CALIFORNIA HIGHWAY PATROL WAS just one of many efforts on the part of California and various other states outside the South to bring about equal rights for African Americans. Although those states did not have the rigid segregation laws of the South, they harbored plenty of racial discrimination. In the late 1950s and early 1960s, the federal government, often under pressure from civil rights groups, also began to take steps to end discriminatory practices and provide more opportunity for black Americans. Senator John F. Kennedy of Massachusetts identified with this goal. After winning election as president of the United States in 1960, Kennedy launched a search for qualified blacks to serve in his administration.

Soon after his inauguration in January 1961, President Kennedy named NAACP attorney Spottswood Robinson to head the federal Civil Rights Commission. Robinson's colleague, Thurgood Marshall, was made a judge on the United States Court of Appeals for the Second Circuit. The Second Circuit covered New York, Connecticut, and Vermont. The U.S. Senate had to confirm this nomination, and southern senators did all they could to block it. Eventually, however, Marshall's appointment was approved by a three-fourths majority of the Senate. Cecil Poole applauded these actions by Kennedy, and he was deeply honored when Kennedy also singled him out for a federal position.

The president asked Poole to serve as United States attorney for the District of Northern California. At the time, California had two districts—northern and southern. Eventually, Congress would create four districts instead of two. In the early 1960s, the Northern District covered an area stretching from the Pacific Ocean to Nevada and from Oregon to just below San Francisco. Appointed for a four-year term, Poole was the first black person in the continental United States to be named a U.S. attorney. "I have the feeling that I'll be operating in a very bright spotlight," he remarked as he paid his first visit to his new office in San Francisco.

As United States attorney, Poole was responsible for representing the government in any legal cases that occurred in that district. That could mean arguing a case before the United States Supreme Court. Lawyers must be "admitted to" the federal courts, including the Supreme Court, before they can argue cases there. William Orrick, who was then an assistant attorney general in the Kennedy administration, made the motion to admit Poole to the nation's highest court, which Chief Justice Earl Warren then accepted. Most of Poole's work, however, was conducted far from the Supreme Court building in the nation's capital.

Poole's new job allowed him to be based once again in San Francisco, where the main office of the U.S. attorney for northern California was located. Poole was as excited as his family to be home again on a regular basis, able to participate in family dinners and pick up his girls from school.

Fourteen-year-old Gayle and nine-year-old Patti were enrolled in the San Francisco public schools. Both their schools were predominantly white, because the Pooles lived in a largely white neighborhood. Had the family lived in a mostly black neighborhood, their children's public schools would have been largely black. The San Francisco schools were not segregated by law, as in the South, but in fact because of housing patterns (this is called *de facto* segregation). Poole didn't like segregation—even if it was *de facto*— and determined to do something about it. He ran successfully for a seat on the school board and in that position did all he could to encourage integration of the schools, primarily through busing. As determined as he was to fight for equity for blacks, however, even he could not change housing patterns.

In addition to the main U.S. attorney's office, Poole had charge of an office in Sacramento. There were two assistant U.S. attorneys in each office, as well as a support staff. Poole made an effort to hire women whenever he could. In those days, women attorneys faced a lot of discrimination and found it far more difficult to get jobs than men. Poole, who had experienced his own share of discrimination because of race, was not about to allow gender to get in the way of important work.

Poole had not been in office long when he realized that the spotlight was going to be on him for more than just his race. Many demonstrations and protests took place outside his office at Seventh and Mission Streets because it represented the U.S. Department of Justice. Among those demonstrations were anti-nuclear protests. Ever since the United States had dropped the first atomic bomb on Hiroshima, Japan, some people had feared a nuclear arms race between the most powerful nations in the world. They worried that the end result would be a third world war. Besides the danger of world war, there was the health risk posed by radioactive fallout from nuclear testing. People who were against nuclear weapons and nuclear testing chose a variety of methods of protest. Some signed petitions and participated in marches, rallies, and demonstrations. Early in Cecil Poole's term as U.S. attorney, major protests took place against nuclear testing on Bikini Atoll in the South Pacific Ocean. Most of those protests took the form of demonstrations outside Poole's office. But one group of protesters went so far as to order a boat built so they could sail it to the target zone.

Robert Kennedy was the U.S. attorney general under his brother President John F. Kennedy. The assistant attorney general was a man named Nicholas Katzenbach. Katzenbach called Poole and told him to get an injunction against the group. Poole disagreed, feeling that it was best to ignore them and that to go after them legally would give their efforts more importance than they deserved. But Katzenbach was afraid the boat would capsize and the group would become martyrs to the anti-nuclear cause. Poole took the request for an injunction to a district judge, who issued an order demanding that the protesters cease and desist until he could call a hearing.

By the time Poole obtained the injunction, the group had already set sail. In fact, they had been gone about three hours. Poole boarded a U.S. Coast Guard cutter, which chased and overtook the protesters' boat. The protesters were arrested and taken into custody. They were suffering from seasickness, and Poole felt sorry for them. When asked to suggest a bail amount for the protesters, Poole suggested $100 per person. He also drew on admiralty law (the rules that govern navigation and shipping) to hold the boat in the government's possession.

The judge at the protesters' hearing was fairly lenient. Only a couple of members of the group spent any time in jail; the rest were let go on the promise not to engage in similar activities in the future. Vacationing with his family in a lakeside cabin in northern California not long afterward, Poole was summoned to a park ranger's office for a telephone call. The protesters who had promised not to use the boat again had been voted out of the group. The others had again set sail for Bikini Atoll. Poole ordered his assistant to have the Coast Guard force the boat to turn around. Remembering that the protesters had been seasick the last time, he told his assistant that they should be forced to remain on the boat until they got back to port.

This time, the government sold the forfeited boat and paid off its builder. The Bikini Atoll protest was only one of several in the years between 1958 and 1962. At least three other vessels tried to sail into nuclear testing sites belonging either to the United States or the Soviet Union.

Another type of protest occurred on Alcatraz Island in San Francisco Bay, the site of a closed federal prison. Beginning in 1969, a group of Native Americans calling themselves Indians of All Tribes decided to occupy the island. Led by activists from the San Francisco Bay Area, they chose Alcatraz to replace the recently burned San Francisco Indian Center. Eventually, Native Americans from across the United States came to join the occupation, which lasted almost two years. The occupiers made a number of demands, including improvement of living conditions on reservations and establishment of an Indian social and education center on the island.

On orders from his superiors, Poole traveled out to the island on a Coast Guard cutter to investigate the situation. He assured the Indians that he had no orders to take them off Alcatraz, only to talk to them. He enjoyed himself, throwing and skipping flat rocks on San Francisco Bay, talking about jazz music, not about the occupation. Then he sailed back to the mainland with a smile on his face. Without saying a word, he assured the Indians on Alcatraz that he had no intentions of moving against them as long as he was in office.

Poole's handling of the Bikini Atoll and Alcatraz Island protests exemplified his independent attitude. Federal judge William Shubb, who worked for a time as an assistant U.S. attorney in the Sacramento office, and later became the U.S. attorney for the Eastern District of California, explains, "Cecil always thought of himself as a presidential appointee. He was there to exercise his judgment about what was just and what ought to be done. He had his own sense of justice. Not to follow the orders of someone in Washington, but to do what he thought he ought to do. There were occasions when he got into a dispute with somebody, and he'd say, 'I've got a piece of paper on my wall that says I make those decisions. The statute says the United States attorney shall represent the United States in all criminal prosecutions and actions on behalf of and against the United States in his district.'

"And if people continued to disagree with him, he'd say, 'Maybe we ought to talk to Bobby,' meaning Bobby Kennedy, the attorney general. And they would back off. I don't know if he was bluffing, but he did have a relationship with Bobby Kennedy."

Poole believed that American law existed to protect the rights of individuals and the right of protest. Those rights were well exercised in the turbulent 1960s, with demonstrations and marches, "takeovers" of university buildings by angry students, "teach-ins" against the Vietnam War, flag-burnings, and attempts to shut down Reserve Officers Training Corps (ROTC) programs. Many colleges and universities had those programs, which trained young men to be officers in the armed forces. By the late 1950s, many students and faculty had come to feel that having ROTC on campus was not compatible with educational aims. In October 1959, an eighteen-year-old University of California student made his opposition known by standing on the steps of one of the university's buildings for several days. Following his example, more and more students began to protest ROTC at the University of California. In 1960, one hundred students demonstrated. The protests by students at the University of California led students at other colleges and universities to demonstrate against ROTC.

Such protests were confined to the North. The southern United States was traditionally more pro-government, at least when it came to defense and the military. The protests that were going on in the South were civil rights actions.

Beginning in 1960, the direct action civil rights movement in the South had heated up. So had the response of white segregationists. Black college students in the South were impatient with the SCLC's and the NAACP's slow and tentative pace of reform. Early in the new decade, college students began to sit in at segregated drugstore lunch counters. Soon black and white students in many parts of the country were engaging in sit-ins to desegregate other public places. A group of those students got together and formed the Student Nonviolent Coordinating Committee (SNCC). In 1961, after the U.S. Supreme Court ruled that segregation in interstate bus terminal restaurants was unconstitutional, the Congress of Racial Equality (CORE) began to test that ruling. CORE, founded in Chicago after World War II, began a series of "Freedom Rides" on interstate buses to the South. When the buses reached the South, angry white mobs stoned the buses and beat the riders.

In 1962, several civil rights organizations combined to force desegregation in Albany, Georgia. But the campaign failed. The following year, Martin Luther King, Jr., and the SCLC organized a similar campaign in Cecil Poole's birthplace—Birmingham, Alabama. In Birmingham, they used a new tactic: Children were sent to desegregate public parks and libraries. The authorities could hardly arrest children, or so local civil rights leaders thought. Television crews and newspaper reporters recorded police hauling children, some no more than seven or eight years old, into vans and off to jail, police clubbing some of the older boys, police and firemen setting dogs and powerful fire hoses against the demonstrators.

Poole recalled the reaction of his two daughters: "At the height of the Birmingham uprising, our two children stared wonderingly at the television set watching Negro children 2,000 miles away shouting Freedom! Freedom! Freedom! as water hoses knocked people down.

"The younger child asked, 'What do they mean by freedom?' The older girl answered for me. 'They mean,' she said, 'that they want to be treated like all people should be treated, and not just like they don't belong here.'

"No words," Poole continued, "could convey more clearly the poignancy, the depth, the sincerity and the simplicity of the Negro's weary search for equality of treatment, of opportunity, of justice, in the land of his birth."

No black person in America was more discouraged by endless talk and inaction than Cecil F. Poole. He could not see how a country with a creed based on what he called "precepts of equality" could not seem to apply those precepts to specific situations, like race relations. There was always too much intellectualization of the race issue—too many studies whose conclusions the nation's leaders did not have the courage to act on. The South was in chaos, but the federal government was failing to take bold steps to reduce tensions and punish bigots and racists who broke the law.

In April 1963, invited to speak to a group of predominantly white high school students at a Youth Conference on Human Rights in Burlingame, California, Poole delivered a blistering attack on what he called racial platitudes and the tendency to study a problem without ever dealing with it. He advised his audience to "commit to memory my particular physiognomy, countenance, stance, inflections, and accents" and explained that "the reason I ask you to remember me is because, in the frustrating and repetitive cycles of human behavior, if your generation does no better than mine in handling its people problems, it will some day end up again and again with someone suggesting that there be yet another study, survey or educational project.

"Now I have nothing against studies, but I figure that if you study me real hard this afternoon, you might end up knowing something about at least one of us—me—and even that little bit of knowledge might save you hours of research later on."

Equally weary but determined not to answer hate with hate, violence with violence, black leaders staged the largest peaceful march on Washington, D.C., in history. The August 1963, the March on Washington for Jobs and Freedom was organized by six civil rights organizations. It brought a quarter of a million blacks and whites to the nation's capital and had a strong impact on President John F. Kennedy, who pledged to work for equal rights laws. It was during that march that Reverend King delivered his famous "I Have a Dream" speech, calling for peace between the races and equality for all people.

But many people in America continued to be consumed by hate. It was a frightening time. The previous April, NAACP field secretary Medgar Evers had been assassinated in Mississippi—the March on Washington had been dedicated to his memory. In September, the Sixteenth Street Baptist Church in Birmingham, Alabama, was bombed, and four young girls lost their lives. In November 1963, President Kennedy was assassinated while riding in a motorcade through the streets of Dallas, Texas.

Poole was in court in Sacramento at the time. It was the first day of a murder case, and Poole was cross-examining a defense witness. One of his staff members caught Poole's eye, and held up a piece of paper. After getting the judge's okay to interrupt his cross-examination to see what the staff member wanted, Poole took the paper and read it. It said, "It is just reported on the radio that President Kennedy was shot while riding in a parade in Dallas. His condition is not known, but blood was seen coming from his head."

Shaken, Poole shared the note with the judge, who immediately adjourned the proceedings. Poole went to the branch office of the U.S. attorney's office in Sacramento and closed the office for the day, leaving one staff member to answer the telephone. He then drove to San Francisco. By the time he reached home, the president had been pronounced dead.

Patti Poole was in sixth grade when President Kennedy was shot. The announcement came while she was playing on the school playground. Her first thought was, "Is my dad going to lose his job?" When she went home, she was surprised to see her father there. It was the first time she had ever seen him cry.

In the midst of his private mourning, Poole had to continue to represent the United States government. The FBI called to ask if he wanted protection, but he declined the offer. He called the Department of Justice in Washington, D.C., and asked if he should attend the funeral. But he was advised to remain in California to assure the smooth workings of his office. He spent the funeral weekend at home, watching the televised events and mourning for the dead president.

"It was hard getting over that, very hard," Poole recalled. "I had met the president on several occasions, and I was just one of ninety-three United States attorneys, but I was absolutely shattered that this had happened to him, and it took me a long, long time to get over it, just a long time." Finally, his wife Charlotte said to him, "You know, I'm the last one that would tell you to go down to your office and do something, but I don't think this is good for you." So Poole got into his car and went to his office and resumed his normal routine.

Not long after President Kennedy's funeral, Poole and the other United States attorneys were summoned to Washington for a meeting to assure a smooth transition after Vice President Lyndon B. Johnson was sworn in as president. President Johnson himself spoke to the assembled group and assured them that the nation's government was continuing to function and that they were to carry on with their jobs. Friction soon developed between Johnson and Attorney General Robert Kennedy, and Kennedy resigned. Johnson replaced him with Nicholas Katzenbach.

President Kennedy had planned to make civil rights a central part of his administration. When Vice President Lyndon B. Johnson succeeded to the presidency, he vowed to carry out the slain president's wishes. Under Johnson, two pieces of landmark federal civil rights legislation were passed—the 1964 Civil Rights Act and the 1965 Voting Rights Act. Together they established the legal basis for equal rights throughout the land. But it would be a long time before white people with racist views would obey those laws. And many more civil rights workers—black and white—were yet to die in the South.

President Johnson reappointed Cecil Poole to another four-year term as U.S. attorney in 1964. By that time, the anti-nuclear movements and the anti-ROTC movements had found a common cause to protest: United States involvement in the war in Vietnam. That conflict between communist North Vietnam and non-communist South Vietnam dated back to the end of World War II, when the country was divided in half. The northern half was controlled by China, the southern half by Great Britain, which soon withdrew in favor of France. After communists took over mainland China, the Western world worried that all of Asia might fall under communist dominance. As early as 1954, President Dwight D. Eisenhower provided aid to South Vietnam. The administration of President John F. Kennedy sent military advisers and huge quantities of weapons. After Kennedy's death in November 1963, President

Johnson ordered the bombing of North Vietnamese shipyards and oil-storage tanks. In March 1965, Johnson announced round-the-clock bombing of North Vietnam.

Although many Americans supported U.S. involvement in the Asian conflict, many others did not. They pointed out that the United States was fighting an undeclared war. Under the U.S. Constitution, only Congress can declare war, and no U.S. president had asked Congress to declare war against North Vietnam. They argued that the conflict between North and South Vietnam was a civil war and the United States had no business interfering. But they were powerless to halt the increasing U.S. military presence in Southeast Asia.

Draft calls were getting larger and larger every month, and thousands of young men were being sent to fight in Vietnam. College students were automatically deferred and allowed to finish college—even graduate school—before serving. If they became teachers, doctors, or scientists, or went into certain other careers, they could avoid the draft altogether. Students, and men in occupations considered important, were thought to be needed at home in the United States.

Ironically, it was college students who began the first major anti-draft protests. They marched against local draft-board offices, city halls, and state legislatures. They sat in and picketed. At the time, every young man had to register with his local draft board when he reached age eighteen. He then received a draft card. It was a crime not to have such a card. But many young men protested the draft by burning their cards or sending them back to the Selective Service System headquarters in Washington, D.C. The anti-draft movement became the most important part of the anti-Vietnam War effort.

Eventually the various protests coalesced into a huge anti-Vietnam War and anti-government movement.

In 1964, the federal government opened a new courthouse on San Francisco's Golden Gate Avenue, many blocks from the old one at Seventh and Mission. This new federal building became a particular target for protests. Almost on a weekly basis, there were marches and demonstrations outside the building.

Judge Charles A. Legge first met Poole after he had left his position as U.S. attorney. He recalls with a chuckle, "We had two great big fountains outside the federal courthouse. The protestors would arrive in great numbers, and they would see those fountains out in front of the courthouse, and they named them 'Cecil's pools.'"

While she was in high school, Patti participated in many anti-war protests. She remembers that when she took part in protests in front of the federal building, "I'd always hang way back in the corner. I knew the FBI was around taking photographs, and I didn't want my dad to see me, although he knew I was there. I didn't want to compromise him." Sometimes, when asked what her father did for a living, she would reply that he was an attorney—with no further explanation.

Only on rare occasions did the protests become violent. Poole remembered a time when the motorcycle gang, the Hell's Angels, threatened to prevent an anti-war demonstration. The Angels supported the government and U.S. involvement in Vietnam. They drove their motorcycles to the scene of the demonstration and began to threaten the protesters. The police had a hard time keeping the two sides apart. It was one of the few times that Poole was really frightened of possible violence.

Occasionally, protesters demanded a meeting in Poole's office. He would not refuse to see them, but he limited the number of people who could visit him to about twenty-five at a time. He expected them to behave appropriately and never forgot his shock when a couple of women wearing spike heels stood on his leather couch.

Once a group staged a protest outside the Poole home. "I came home from a guitar lesson one Saturday, and they were picketing our house," Patti Poole remembers. "I knew one of the guys in the picket line; he was a friend of a friend in high school. I asked why he was doing this. I said, 'This is my dad's house, for God's sake! Picket the Federal Building, but don't picket the house! Why are you disturbing my father at home?' And then my mother came out and scolded, 'Patricia, don't you talk to them!' and dragged me back inside."

Being the target of demonstrations was the least of U.S. Attorney Poole's problems. Far more burdensome were the draft violator cases his office was expected to prosecute. Many young American men of draft age protested the draft by avoiding it altogether. They fled to Canada. They went underground. They failed to register, or they registered using a false address. If called, they refused to report for induction or for physical examinations. Such methods of avoiding the draft did not sit well with most people in the country, including members of Congress. They expected vigorous prosecution of Selective Service violators.

Poole started trying to prosecute them, but he soon found that many of the cases were not strong enough. Local draft boards were composed of ordinary citizens who were not experts in documenting a draft violation. Often the documentation provided by local draft boards in California was not enough for legal prosecution. For example, one young man registered at the time of his eighteenth birthday. Notified to appear for a physical examination, he did not show up. The draft board reported him to Poole's office as a Selective Service violator. But to prosecute him, the U.S. attorney's office needed proof that the young man had received the notice for the physical examination and had deliberately failed to respond to it. That meant having proof that he still lived at the address to which the notice had been sent. Often, the draft board did not have that proof. Most judges would throw out such cases for insufficient evidence. In the event that a trial began and then a judge threw out the case, the violator could never be charged for the same crime again. The rule of law called "double jeopardy" prevented him from being tried a second time.

Poole set up a special team in his office to handle Selective Service violations. Its first duty was to study the documentation the draft board provided. When that documentation was found to be incomplete, Poole's office would send the papers back to the draft board. After draft boards began complaining to the state director of Selective Service, Poole was summoned to Washington, D.C., to discuss the matter with General Lewis B. Hershey, director of the Selective Service System.

When Poole explained his reasons for sending cases back to the local draft boards, Hershey replied, "But a lot of people don't understand that, and it doesn't sell well." Poole recalled saying to him, "Look, I tell you what, if you feel this way, why don't you come down to San Francisco and tell the judges how you feel, because they're the ones who have to make the decisions." When General

Hershey replied that he wasn't going to tell the judges what to do, Poole said to him, "Neither am I."

While in Washington, D.C., Poole met with officials at the Department of Justice and explained the procedures he had established and the reason so many cases were sent back to the local draft boards. U.S. Attorney General Ramsey Clark and others at Justice understood the legalities. Non-lawyers did not.

Once word got out that Poole was "soft on draft evaders," his office's caseload grew even larger. Young men traveled to California to violate the Selective Service rules. "It was sapping my strength," Poole recalled. "I didn't have enough people to handle it. These were pretty hectic times."

According to Jerrold Ladar, Poole's management style did not help in easing the backlog of cases. "Cecil was terrible about answering phone calls. He'd just decide he wasn't going to. It wouldn't be any one person in particular—just across the board. He also had a theory that the way you know what is going on in an office—if you are at the top—is to look at all the mail, at what is coming in and going out. So we would take the mail up so he could see what it was. But we found at a certain point, if he was getting busy, the mail would stack up, and your stuff that you thought went out Monday went out on Wednesday. People would call and ask if we'd received their letter, and it would be up in one of the piles in Cecil's office.

"But when he was ready to do correspondence, he could do it with great efficiency. He could dictate letters that were absolutely perfect in structure and grammar. He was articulate," Ladar recalled, "and he could turn a phrase like nobody's business. His secretary would take it down and type it up, and there would be no need for revisions."

* * * * *

In all his years as a practicing attorney, Poole had never become a member of the American Bar Association. Nevertheless, when he was invited to speak at an ABA convention in 1966, his colleagues urged him to accept the invitation. The ABA had changed greatly since 1939, when it had rejected Poole's application because the group did not accept black members. The organization was doing the best it could to overcome its sorry past, but it was still having trouble attracting minority members. A new Section on Individual Rights had been created, and Poole was asked to join this section as well as the Criminal Law Section.

With some misgivings, Poole accepted the ABA's invitations and joined the organization at last. He did not regret his decision. He eventually served as chairman of the Section on Individual Rights and helped to found the Section on Litigation, which became one of the largest.

By 1966, the nation was so focused on the Vietnam War and the anti-war movement that, in Poole's opinion, most white people had simply forgotten about civil rights. That concerned him, because he knew there was much more to be done. Even though federal legislation now existed that was meant to guarantee equal rights, many years would pass before the effects of that legislation were felt at the grassroots level. In the meantime, many of the people who had sat in and marched and ridden on buses through the South in the direct-action civil rights movement were tired of the nonviolent struggle. Scores of people had been beaten and threatened. Some had lost their lives. Many were bitter and tired of the nonviolent way. Stokely Carmichael, the new president of the Student

Nonviolent Coordinating Committee, insisted it was time for new tactics, and in 1966 he issued a call for "Black Power!"

The direct-action civil rights movement had been focused on the South, where legalized segregation was a clear target. Not so easy to fight was the kind of discrimination that occurred outside the South. In many parts of the country, life was also deeply segregated, although there were no laws decreeing it. Blacks in northern and western cities saw no change in their lives as a result of the direct-action civil rights movement. A new black militancy was arising in those cities. Even traditionally moderate groups like the NAACP were beset by infighting, usually between younger, more militant members and older, more moderate ones. In the San Francisco branch of the NAACP, a major dispute concerned the proper role of political activity in the black protest movement. This dispute created a rift between the political and protest leaders in the city. The chapter's president, Dr. Thomas Burbridge, believed that high NAACP office holders should not also hold important political office in the community. He and his supporters felt that the ability of these office holders to protest the actions of local government was compromised because they were part of it. Poole, who was a member of the chapter's board of directors, disagreed. He felt it was best to work for change within the system. He agreed with Dr. Carlton B. Goodlett, the prominent black physician, newspaper owner, and long-time NAACP member and officer, who once said, "The black tail is never going to wag the white dog. But if we live in the belly of the beast, we can cause quite a bellyache."

Both Poole and Goodlett had supported the political aspirations of Willie Brown, a young black attorney who had gone into private practice after being unable to find a position with one of the city's white law firms. Brown had joined the National Urban League and the Young Democrats as well as the NAACP. Although his first attempt at winning a seat in the state assembly in 1962 was unsuccessful, he won the seat two years later. He was re-elected sixteen times and served for thirty-one years, fifteen of them as speaker of the assembly. He was the first black to serve as speaker, a position second only to that of the governor. Passage of state term limits in 1990 effectively ended Brown's term as speaker (some people believed the law was specially designed to end his long political career), but in 1995 he won election as San Francisco's first black mayor.

To Burbridge and his supporters, however, being in the belly of the beast meant being digested by the system. Willie Brown's election to the assembly in November 1964 did not change their minds. When election for NAACP offices was held in December 1964, Burbridge and his people won. Poole was denied a seat on the board of directors.

Meanwhile, another form of black militancy was arising in the San Francisco area. In the fall of 1966, two students at Oakland City College named Huey Newton and Bobby Seale established the Black Panther Party for Self-Defense. Far from accepting the concept of non-violence, they believed that blacks had every right to defend themselves from racism and brutality. Newton expressed his views when he explained the choice of a name for the new organization: "The nature of the panther is that he never attacks. But if anyone attacks him or backs him into a corner, that panther comes up to wipe that aggressor or attacker out, absolutely, resolutely, wholly, thoroughly, and completely."

In October 1966, Newton and Seale completed the party's ten-point platform, entitled "What We Want, What We Believe." Among the wants were freedom, full employment, decent housing, education, exemption of black men from military service, an end to police brutality, release of all black men from the nation's prisons and jails, and an opportunity for blacks to vote on their national destiny. Quoting from the Declaration of Independence, the platform called for a new, black revolution.

Newton and Seale chose a novel way to announce the existence of the Black Panther Party. On May 2, 1967, Seale led a group of thirty Panthers, all dressed in blue shirts, black berets, and black leather jackets, to the steps of the capitol building in Sacramento. (Newton was not with the group because he was on parole from prison, where he had served six months for a knife fight, and was certain he would be re-imprisoned as a result.) The twenty-four men in the group carried loaded rifles. The women were unarmed. The group entered the capitol and made their way to the assembly room where the Mulford Act, a gun-control bill, was being debated. Their appearance caused chaos, and they were ordered into a hallway. There, amid the popping of flashbulbs and wild scrambling on the part of reporters, Seale read a prepared message that called on black people to arm themselves against racist police agencies.

Seale put the police on notice, and the authorities responded as expected. Not just the local police, but agents of the Federal Bureau of Investigation began monitoring Panther activities. Eventually, the Panthers were in a virtual war with law enforcement authorities.

Poole did not consider himself an enemy of the Panthers, as long as they did not break the law. He managed to keep the lines of communication open with them, although he was skeptical of their tactics, and they dismissed what they considered his antiquated thinking. He disapproved of the efforts by city, state, and federal law enforcement officials to break the Panthers. When asked why by those officials, he responded, "Well, because there's a little thing in the Constitution of the United States about the right of people to seek redress from the government, and that kind of thing."

But Poole was virtually alone among law enforcement officials. In late October 1967, a shootout between police and Panthers in Oakland resulted in Newton's arrest. Six months later, in April 1968, another shootout in Oakland claimed the life of seventeen-year-old Panther Bobby Hutton. By late fall of that year, FBI director J. Edgar Hoover was declaring the Panthers "the greatest threat to the internal security of the country."

Whether U.S. Attorney Cecil F. Poole could have made a difference in the sad story of the Black Panther Party versus the government is unknown, because he never had the opportunity to try. In spite, or perhaps because, of all the progress the nation had made in offering equal opportunity to all its citizens, race relations in the United States had reached a level of violence that had not been seen since the lynching era. That climate of hatred claimed Dr. Martin Luther King, Jr., in April 1968, when he died from an assassin's bullet in Memphis, Tennessee, where he had gone to support a black garbage workers' strike.

In early spring 1968, not long before King's assassination, President Johnson announced that he would not seek re-election as president. He was the most hated president in years, due primarily to his conduct of the Vietnam War. Hardly anyone, it seemed, remembered how much he had done for black Americans. During his first years in office, he had honored President Kennedy's pledge to make civil rights for blacks a major focus of his administration. Under Johnson, two landmark pieces of legislation had been enacted: the 1964 Civil Rights Act and the 1965 Voting Rights Act. Johnson had also undertaken a massive anti-poverty program, which he called The Great Society. This program had introduced Head Start, free school lunches, job training, and affirmative action efforts to help lift poor people, especially minorities, onto a level playing field with whites. But all those actions on the home front were overshadowed by his buildup of U.S. forces in Vietnam. The anti-war movement brought down Lyndon Baines Johnson.

Once Johnson announced he would not run, Vice President Hubert Humphrey seemed the likely Democratic candidate for president. But Robert Kennedy, who had served as U.S. attorney general in the administration of his brother, John F. Kennedy, launched his own campaign for the Democratic presidential nomination. He was on a campaign stop in Los Angeles when he was assassinated. Cecil Poole had privately supported Kennedy's candidacy, and he was nearly as devastated by his death as he had been by that of the former president.

President Johnson, like Kennedy before him, had been determined to appoint black Americans to federal government positions. In 1965, he had made Thurgood Marshall the first black solicitor general of the United States. Sometimes called the tenth member of the U.S. Supreme Court, the solicitor general is the chief courtroom lawyer for the executive branch and also has offices at the Supreme Court. The solicitor general decides which cases from federal agencies should go to the Supreme Court and which are not worthy of the Court's time. Marshall's appointment was confirmed by the Senate, and he was sworn in on August 24, 1965. On June 13, 1967, less than two years later, Johnson appointed Marshall the first black justice on the U.S. Supreme Court, and the Senate confirmed that appointment.

Poole was not so fortunate. He lost the chance to be appointed a United States district judge because of his insistence on prosecuting only draft cases with strong and complete evidence (which some viewed as evidence that he was "soft on draft evaders"). In 1966, when new federal courts were established in San Jose and Oakland, he emerged as the frontrunner for the position of U.S. district court judge. Robert F. Peckham, one-time assistant United States attorney and later a Santa Clara County superior court judge, was soon named to the San Jose post. The judgeship in Oakland proved more problematic to fill. The Northern California District was represented by six Democratic congressmen, who got together and proposed Poole and Alameda County Superior Court Judge Lionel J. Wilson, who was also black, to President Johnson.

The way the system worked was that when a new judgeship or a vacancy occurred, the president consulted with the senators of the state in question, and they recommended a nominee. The names of nominees were sent to the U.S. Department of Justice for background checks by the FBI. At the time, the American Bar Association's Standing Committee on the Federal Judiciary also had a role in the process. Members of that committee called twenty to fifty people from different segments of the legal profession for their opinions and also read any legal writings of the nominees, then rated the nominees as "highly qualified," "qualified," or "unqualified" (the administration of President George W. Bush discontinued the practice of consulting the ABA).

The FBI check on Poole's background apparently unearthed nothing suspicious, for his name was sent to the ABA's Standing Committee on the Federal Judiciary. There, however, he ran into trouble. For all its attempts to be more inclusive, the ABA was still a predominantly white organization and still contained a lot of racism. Poole nearly fell victim to racism on the committee. Citing an occasion in which Poole had gotten into a heated argument with a judge, the committee at first turned him down, citing "lack of judicial temperament." But Albert Jenner, chairman of the committee, and Bernard Segal, the former chairman, persuaded the committee to change its mind. Jenner was so determined that he actually wrote a sixty-eight-page legal brief in support of Poole. The committee eventually rated Poole as "qualified."

The way now seemed clear for Poole. He even traveled to Washington, D.C., to have his photograph taken with President Johnson. But the photograph was never released because the appointment was withdrawn. As congratulatory telegrams and telephone calls poured in, Senator George Murphy, Republican of California, managed to block Poole's appointment.

On January 9, 1968, Lyndon B. Johnson re-nominated Poole to be a federal district judge and forwarded the nomination to the Senate Judiciary Committee, but it was not acted on. That committee was too busy dealing with the controversy over another of Johnson's judicial appointments—the failed nomination of Abe Fortas as chief justice of the United States. With a presidential election looming, Poole knew there would be no further movement on his appointment until the nation had chosen a new occupant for the White House.

In the 1968 presidential election, Vice President Hubert Humphrey, a Democrat from Minnesota, ran against former Vice President Richard Nixon of California. Humphrey was well liked, but his association with the Johnson administration, the war in Vietnam, and the chaos caused by the anti-war movement hurt his campaign. Nixon's running mate, Spiro T. Agnew of Maryland, caught the attention of the press and public by portraying Humphrey's supporters as "that effete corps of impudent snobs." In one speech, Agnew called Democrats "nattering nabobs of negativism." Today, we'd call Agnew's heavily critical language "going negative." Agnew's flamboyant, colorful style of portraying political opponents helped Nixon, whose own style was much more reserved or "statesmanlike."

Nixon and Agnew vowed to bring about an honorable end to the war. They also stressed the need to end the turmoil that gripped the nation. Their platform stressed "law and order," by which they meant a crackdown on the protests that had roiled the country. They had no sympathy for the anti-war movement and did not support continued civil rights protests. Poole was skeptical of their law-and-order campaign. He knew, as many in the public apparently did not, that maintaining order is the responsibility of state and local law enforcement agencies, not the federal government. And he firmly believed that cracking down on the anti-war movement would threaten national security.

Nixon and Agnew won the election in November 1968 and took over the White House in late January 1969. It is customary for all pending federal nominations to be withdrawn when a new president takes office, especially when the incoming administration is of a different political party. Poole's was one of 155 federal nominations to be withdrawn so President Nixon could review them. Poole, a lifelong Democrat, was not re-nominated. As was customary, President Nixon appointed Republicans and friends of the Republican Party to posts in his administration. Poole remained in office as U.S. attorney almost a full year after Nixon was inaugurated. But Senator George Murphy was anxious that he be removed, and

Poole knew his days in a government position were numbered. For the first time in more than twenty years, Cecil Poole was about to be a private citizen.

Through his friend and associate William Coblentz, one of the regents, or board members, of the University of California, Poole was invited to be a regents' professor at Boalt Hall, the law school at Berkeley. He tied up as many loose ends as he could in his busy office and then, in December, called a news conference to announce his resignation. He did not know that only a few hours earlier, President Nixon had appointed someone to replace him. As reporters assembled for the press conference, Poole joked with them, as he usually did. His humor had a decided edge. Referring to one of the memorable campaign slogans delivered by Vice President Agnew, he told reporters, "I'm changing my registration from Democratic to effete, impudent snob." Asked if he could be quoted, he grinned, "Sure, you can tape it. If you're suggesting there is some caution I should exercise now, it's too late." He also said on the record for the first time that his nomination for a federal judgeship had been blocked by Senator George Murphy and that he felt he had been unfairly and unjustly treated. He insisted, however, that he was not bitter, saying, "You have to learn to live with yourself and not let them break you. But it was a disappointment."

Poole knew that he had left his mark. He had presided over the office of United States attorney for the Northern District of California during some of the greatest turmoil of the 1960s and pursued justice as fairly and equitably as he could. He had affected a great variety of people. Among them was William Shubb, who had joined the U.S. attorney's office in Sacramento during Poole's tenure. "I worked directly under Cecil for two years," Judge Shubb recalls.

"But I learned enough from him in that two years to be my guiding principles for the remaining time I worked in the U.S. attorney's office. Every time I had a new problem, I would think, well, how would Cecil handle this? And that would be how I would answer the problem. Then in 1980 I was appointed U.S. attorney in Sacramento, for the Eastern District of California. And still, when I had a problem, I would think, what would Cecil do?

"We stayed in touch. Every year, around Thanksgiving, all the former U.S. attorneys and assistant U.S. attorneys would get together for dinner in San Francisco. Cecil would always come to that and he always dominated it—he and the lawyers who worked for him. All of the spirit that had developed was in that period of time. We'd get together and tell anecdotes, but we always saved Cecil for last. Cecil would get up and talk like a father figure. He used to say that he didn't realize until after he left the job how much power we had over other people's lives. During the time he was in private practice he didn't have that power."

Cecil Poole's return to private life gave him more time to pursue his
hobby of photography.

CHAPTER 9

BACK IN PRIVATE LIFE

AT BOALT HALL, POOLE LECTURED AND CONDUCTED SEMINARS. It was not his first time teaching. Back when he was an assistant district attorney, he had taught evening classes at Golden Gate University's main campus in downtown San Francisco. At Boalt Hall years later, he was astonished at the irreverence of the students. He had been so in awe of his professors at Harvard Law School. Even at Golden Gate, the students had been very respectful. But the students at Golden Gate had been older, most of them with jobs. Those at Boalt Hall were young and often impudent. Still, he enjoyed the challenge of matching wits with them.

When William Coblentz found a place for Poole at his law firm, Poole left teaching without regret. He was more comfortable in the real world of law. Besides, teaching did not pay very well. Poole later joked that after he joined the Coblentz firm he no longer had to look at his wallet before he went out. Nevertheless, he would gladly have accepted a lower salary if he had been appointed a district judge. Several influential people believed that he had been unfairly denied the federal appointment and continued to work behind the scenes on his behalf. William Orrick, a San Francisco attorney who had served in the Justice Department during the Johnson administration, approached Richard Kleindienst, deputy attorney general in the Nixon administration, and tried to persuade him to submit Poole's name as a candidate for that court. But Poole had had run-ins with Attorney General John Mitchell over prosecuting police brutality in San Francisco, which would prevent Mitchell's acceptance of Poole's appointment. As long as Nixon was in the White House and Mitchell was his attorney general, Poole didn't even pay attention to whether there were any vacancies on the district court. He concentrated on his private law practice.

When he first joined the firm of Jacobs, Sills & Coblentz, Poole took on cases that were already in progress. Because he was an experienced litigator, or trial lawyer, Poole was called on to handle cases that seemed to be headed to court. Robert Gordon, who shared an office suite with Poole at the firm, asked him to litigate matters involving some of his clients from the music business including the Doobie Brothers, the Jefferson Airplane, and members of the band Santana. Later, when Poole became a district judge, Gordon gave Poole a platinum Doobie Brothers record album plaque that read "To the Honorable Cecil F. Poole, for selling a million records." The plaque caught many visitors' attention when they saw it in Poole's chambers.

Gordon recalled that Poole was a "wonderful, personable guy," who was conscientious about his work. Not long after they met, Gordon casually asked Poole if he knew about a small point of law he was working on. "I thought maybe off the top of his head he'd say a few words," Gordon remembered. Instead, Poole got up from his desk, went across the hall to the firm's library, researched the point thoroughly, and came back a couple of hours later with the answer. The two men became fast friends after that, and spent much social time together.

Among William Coblentz's clients was Bill Graham, owner of the Fillmore (later the Fillmore West) and Winterland Ballroom, a rock music concert hall that became legendary in the 1960s for its presentations of the Grateful Dead, the Doors, and other groups. The story goes that someone brought a tub of Kool-Aid laced with LSD to a Grateful Dead concert at the Fillmore and that half the audience went home high on "acid." Sued by unhappy parents, Graham called Coblentz, who asked Poole to handle the case. Poole successfully argued in court that Graham's security guards did not know about the tub of acid-laced Kool-Aid until it was too late to prevent unsuspecting members of the audience from drinking it. Graham was so appreciative that he began referring his friends to Poole.

Patti recalls that her father consulted with Graham and the Rolling Stones in a civil suit brought by relatives of a man allegedly killed by the Hell's Angels, the security force for the band's free concert at Altamont Speedway in December 1969. Instead of keeping the peace, the motorcycle gang, which had been hired by the Stones at the suggestion of the Grateful Dead's manager, fought with one another and with the crowd. The Stones were into their fourth song when the first altercation occurred. Mick Jagger repeatedly interrupted the band's performance, begging the crowd to calm down. About three songs later, another fight broke out near the front of the stage. This time a man was killed. Poole advised Graham and the Stones about how to resolve the lawsuit equitably.

Poole frequently asked his daughter Patti to serve as his messenger in his dealings with Bill Graham and other rock scene clients. "Dad often sent me to Winterland or Fillmore West when he had to have documents signed by Bill," she says. "He could never pin him down during the day. He'd ask if I wanted to see a concert, and when I said yes, he'd say, 'Take these papers with you.'" Patti's identification badge gave her access to all the exclusive backstage areas where she would eventually find Graham, as well as meet and interact with musicians and others.

While in private practice, Poole was able to renew his ties with various civil rights and legal organizations. He had served as a director of the NAACP Legal Defense and Educational Fund since the time of Thurgood Marshall's appointment to the United States Supreme Court. This fund, which had become a separate entity from the main NAACP, had dozens of lawsuits in progress, and as a director, Poole helped raise money and advised on legal matters. He became a trustee of the National Urban League, formed the year after the NAACP to help southern blacks who had moved to northern cities. He also continued his work with the American Bar Association. Around 1971, he was invited to join the board of directors of the Levi Strauss Company, the venerable blue jeans manufacturer in San Francisco.

In the meantime, the tumultuous events of the 1960s spilled over into the new decade. In spite of his desire to bring about an end to the war in Vietnam through a negotiated settlement, President Nixon found himself pursuing the war as had his predecessor. Only after he ordered invasions of Cambodia in 1970 and Laos in 1971 was he able to achieve a cease-fire. The anti-war movement continued, as did the violent response to it on the part of law enforcement officers. In 1970, Ohio National Guardsmen fired on student protesters at Kent State University, killing four young people.

A severe nationwide economic recession caused the Nixon administration to impose a wide-ranging system of wage and price controls in 1971. They were not as stringent as those Poole had helped oversee when he was with the Office of Price Administration after World War II, but he could not help remembering that time.

As a private citizen, Poole could be openly aligned with a political party. He had always been a Democrat, but now he could get involved in the work of the party. In 1972, he served on the Credentials Committee, which held hearings on the diversity of the state delegations to the party's convention in Miami, Florida. Four years earlier, the Democratic National Convention in Chicago, Illinois, had been disrupted by protesters who charged that there were not enough women, minorities, or youth in the state delegations. Senator George McGovern of South Dakota had then chaired a reform commission, which established a process by which complaints about the diversity of a delegation could be made and heard.

In addition to serving on the Credentials Committee, Poole chaired a hearing about the Illinois delegation, which numbered about seventy-five men, nearly all of whom were city officials—aldermen and other politicians. The Reverend Jesse Jackson was directing a Chicago organization called Operation PUSH at the time. Jackson, a former member of the Southern Christian Leadership Conference, had worked with Dr. Martin Luther King, Jr., and was a firm believer in integration. He described Operation PUSH as a "rainbow coalition of blacks and whites gathered together to push for a greater share of economic and political power for all poor people in America in the spirit of Dr. Martin Luther King, Jr." He and other blacks in Chicago were furious that all the members of the Illinois delegation were white males, and they filed a complaint with the Credentials Committee. Patricia Roberts Harris, chair of the committee, asked Poole to fly to Chicago to hold a hearing on the complaint.

Harris had warned him that the hearing might get vicious, and once in Chicago Poole realized what she was talking about. Try as he might, he could not get the members of the Illinois delegation to stop talking so the hearing could proceed. Things got pretty rowdy, and Poole realized the little gavel he was pounding on his table was useless. He finally announced that nothing was getting done and if he didn't have quiet he would simply take all the written complaints back home to California, read them in peace, and make his decision. That threat worked, and the hearing went on in an orderly manner for three days.

In his official report, Poole wrote that the Illinois delegation had violated every one of the rules of conduct set forth by the 1968 McGovern commission. He recommended that the entire delegation be barred from official Democratic Party activity.

Although the 1972 Democratic Convention in Miami was the party's most diverse in history, that did not help the party's presidential candidate, Senator George McGovern, in the election. In spite of his problems with the Vietnam War and the American economy, Republican President Richard Nixon won re-election to the presidency that year in a landslide victory. Re-elected along with him was Vice President Agnew. But the following year, Agnew was forced to resign amidst charges of corruption dating back to when he was a Baltimore, Maryland, county executive. Congressman

Gerald R. Ford was nominated to the vice presidency by Nixon and confirmed by both houses of Congress, as provided by the Twenty-Fifth Amendment to the Constitution. Coincidentally, Ford had been captain of the University of Michigan football team when Poole was a freshman there.

In 1974, after the turmoil known as "Watergate," Ford became president. Back in 1972, burglars hired by Richard Nixon's campaign committee had broken into the offices of the Democratic National Committee in the Watergate apartment complex in Washington, D.C., looking for information that would help Nixon's campaign. President Nixon and his closest advisers tried to cover up their connection to the burglary, but the story leaked out to the news media. Faced with mounting evidence that he had authorized the cover-up, Nixon resigned. Poole was delighted to see him go. Vice President Ford served out the remaining two years of Nixon's four-year term.

During the two years that Ford served as president, a vacancy occurred on the U.S. District Court for Northern California. California's Democratic senators John Tunney and Alan Cranston proposed Poole for the judgeship, and President Ford agreed to nominate him. When Senator Cranston called Poole to tell him that he had been nominated, Cecil and Charlotte were preparing to fly to Rio de Janiero for Carnival. Ordinarily, Poole was too busy to take a vacation, but a trial in which he was involved was halted for three weeks. As soon as he told Charlotte that he had three weeks off, she went to a travel agent and booked airline tickets and a hotel reservation. After the call from Cranston, Poole knew he couldn't take that trip, but he was not yet ready to tell his wife the reason. He simply told her that there was too much going on for him to leave the country for three weeks. She agreed to cancel the trip. Instead, they went to the Kona Village Resort in Hawaii for six days.

Poole intended to talk to Charlotte about the judicial nomination while they were on vacation. But he was having a hard time making up his mind about it. Having been disappointed twice before, he was reluctant to get his hopes up. He also enjoyed what he was doing—and the money he was making. When he finally told Charlotte, he admitted that he didn't know what to do. "The hell you don't," she answered. "After all these years, you've never gotten over what happened when Nixon withdrew your nomination and all that." Poole knew she was right. "I did have these feelings," he admitted years later. "I felt that, for many reasons, symbolically there was almost no escape for me. Nobody would understand what I meant if I said I don't want to do it."

Poole's chances were much improved this time around because his nomination was part of a three-nominee package for three judicial vacancies. Once again, Poole went through the vetting process: the FBI background check and the ABA Standing Committee on the Federal Judiciary decision. He passed both with flying colors. President Ford approved the three judicial nominations, which then went to the Senate Judiciary Committee for confirmation hearings.

At Poole's hearing, one of the senators asked if he understood that it was the function of Congress to make the laws and that judges should not, by their decisions, try to enact legislation that Congress had not intended. Poole responded that there were very few judges who really believed it was their function to enact or change the law. He added that very often judges found themselves having to make decisions on matters that legislators had shied away from. The committee voted for him and the full Senate confirmed Poole's nomination. His commission was dated July 1976—a fitting time, the bicentennial of the Declaration of Independence. That same year, according to statistics, the number of black students enrolled in law schools across the country had increased to 4.7 percent, up from just 1 percent in 1965.

It was three months before Poole took the oath of office as a U.S. District Court judge. Jacobs, Sills & Coblentz was a fairly small firm, and Poole was in the midst of cases he could not simply abandon. He had to bring them to some sort of conclusion first. Poole's formal induction ceremony took place in the ceremonial courtroom in San Francisco's federal building. In attendance were the sitting judges of the United States District Court, several senior (retired) judges of the District Court, judges from other courts, including the United States Court of Appeals and the California Supreme Court, two congressmen from the San Francisco area, former Governor Edmund "Pat" Brown, Senators Alan Cranston and John Tunney, and Poole's family and friends.

Among the speakers was Warren Christopher, who in 1993 would become President Bill Clinton's secretary of state. Christopher attended the ceremony as chairman of the American Bar Association's Standing Committee on the Federal Judiciary. In his remarks, Christopher noted that although there was no legal basis for it, the ABA's committee had for the past twenty years been consulted by presidents with respect to most judicial appointments. "I am delighted to tell this Court, tell the audience," said Christopher, "that Judge Poole came through what we regard as a rigorous test with flying colors.

"As chairman," he went on, "I have made an informal study of the period of time between nomination and swearing in. It is an interesting study, because it tells you something about how long it takes a man to get out of his practice, how long a vacation he can afford to take. And I have to say that studying the time between Cecil's first nomination and this swearing in ceremony, he is going to go down in the Guinness Book of Records. . . . Don't you think eight years is a little long, Cecil?"

Of course everyone knew that it was not Poole's fault, but the nature of politics, that kept him from joining the court the first time he was nominated. By contrast, politics could not be blamed for the fact that it had taken Poole three months to leave his private practice and join the court.

William Coblentz began his remarks, "Chief Judge Peckham, members of the Court, I can now reveal to this Court, as well as to this audience, a hitherto secret, unpublished document. It is called the retroactive judicial evaluation of Judge Cecil F. Poole. Now, let me, if I may, read in part some of this document. First, promptness in being sworn in: Excellent, 5 percent. Satisfactory, 10 percent. Unsatisfactory, 85 percent. Chief Judge Peckham has asked that he specifically be included in this poll. Second, perseverance or persistence or, in other words, if you don't succeed, try, try again: Excellent, 100 percent."

When it came time for Poole to speak, he thanked his family and the many friends in attendance. "No one really walks alone," he continued, "and each of us needs to have the mutual warmth and affection, sustenance and support, encouragement and criticism that come from those who are near and dear to them."

Poole then talked about his future as a judge. He recalled his time working in the office of Governor Brown, saying, "When he was appointing judges, he always tried to make a personal telephone call to them. And when he told them that he intended to appoint them, he invariably said that he was confident of that person's professional standing, capacity, and mind, but that he wanted above all for the person as a judge to remember that he was dealing with people and with their lawyers, both of whom are often in error; and that kindness and understanding and compassion would go a lot further in the cause of justice than sheer brilliance. . . . I would like to be that kind of judge."

U.S. District Judge Poole with Andrew Young, then mayor of Atlanta, Georgia, 1970s

CHAPTER 10

U.S. District Judge Poole

WHEN HE PUT ON HIS BLACK JUDGE'S ROBES FOR THE FIRST time, Poole felt uncomfortable and strangely unprepared. He was sixty-two years old and had practiced law for more than thirty-five years. More times than he could count, he had told himself that he could do a better job than the judge before whom he was arguing. But sitting in the judge's seat was a lot different from daydreaming about it. Years later, Poole recalled with laughter that his first utterance as a judge was not exactly solemn and formal.

He entered the courtroom, the bailiff said, "All rise," and everyone in the room stood up. Poole sat down, everyone else took his seat, and then he looked down at the defendant and said, "I guess you're my first customer." That defendant had been charged with a minor narcotics offense. The government prosecutor wanted Poole to impose a stiff sentence. The defense attorney asked for a lighter one—two years. Poole sentenced the man to two years. That defendant later gave him a statue of Justice with her scales, inscribed with the words "Your first customer." He also wrote to Poole from time to time. In later years, guidelines were established that prevented such communications between judges and defendants.

Judges were paid around the first of the month. About three weeks after his induction, Poole received his first paycheck. He did a double-take when he saw the amount. When he realized that the check represented his monthly salary, he wondered why anyone went to so much trouble to secure a federal judgeship. He said as much to Charlotte when he went home that night, but she just laughed. A United States judgeship might carry great honor, but it does not pay nearly as well as private legal practice.

The job required another sacrifice. Just as when he had served as a United States attorney, Poole had to give up some of his outside activities. He resigned from the board of the Levi Strauss Company and from other corporate boards and organizations. He regretted having to do this, because he had enjoyed working alongside other business and civic leaders. But, like the small paycheck, resigning from those boards went with the territory. Not only judges but also their wives must refrain from engaging in any activity that might be construed as a conflict of interest. Thus Charlotte Poole also had to give up positions on various boards and cut back on her political activities. Says Judge Charles Legge of Charlotte, "She was a great talent going untapped. U.S. judges are by law limited to what they can do. We can't endorse political candidates, we can't go to political speeches, we can't give money to political parties. That neutralizes us—and our wives. I had a feeling with Charlotte that there was a real intellect that was not being used. She was devoting her life to her role of wife and mother and being Cecil's support, and it showed a lot with Cecil."

Despite the politics involved in selecting federal judges, and despite having to give up community and business memberships on corporate and organization boards (which often pay well), most federal judges do a good job. As Poole once explained, "The federal court system operates on a pretty high plane. . . . [U]nlike the state system where you do have the state supreme court as a monitor for keeping the law straight, the importance of the rulings is much, much stronger in the federal system, because eventually a precedent may be created which will affect other states and other things as well. Federal judges make decisions that have a major effect on public policy and thus on American society. When a person takes a seat on the federal bench, the sense of responsibility outweighs the politics that may have gone on before."

Poole enjoyed presiding over the trials of cases, being part of justice in action. From that first visit so many years before with his father, he had always liked being in the courtroom. "I liked jury trials," he later explained. "They were interesting—to listen to the witnesses and see what lawyers were on their feet, whether they knew what they were doing, which ones you wouldn't want for free."

Patti Poole says, "He had experience in all kinds of law, which is what made him a good district judge. And he wouldn't take anything from the attorneys. He would throw attorneys out if they weren't prepared—if they came in with an ill-written brief, he'd tell them to go back and do it again. He did that to one of his own clerks, as a matter of fact; she came in and was unprepared and he said, 'Come back next week.'"

Poole heard a great variety of cases. One he remembered in particular was a civil case concerning the commercial process of ripening fruit. Bananas that are imported to the United States, for example, are picked in Central America when they are still green and shipped to large processing plants to be ripened. An individual had developed a new method of speeding the ripening process by using a kind of gas. Some of his competitors were concerned with the danger of gas explosion and advised their distributors not to use the method. The developer of the process then sued one of the competitors for slander.

The defendant insisted that some people on the East Coast had been hurt in gas explosions, but when pressed for proof, he was unable to call any witnesses. Poole recessed the case for a couple of days to allow time to find those witnesses. When the time was up, he ruled that the trial must proceed. The case went to the jury, which found that the competitor had engaged in willful slander. The jury also awarded a substantial financial settlement to the plaintiff. Poole was not surprised that the jury had found the defendant guilty of slander, because no witnesses had been produced to prove injury from exploding gas. He was surprised at the amount of the financial penalty the jury assessed.

Just days later, the attorney for the losing side contacted him and said he now had proof that the explosions on the East Coast had indeed taken place. He believed that this proof had been suppressed. He asked Poole to delay the judgment. Poole said he would do so only if the losing side paid for the plaintiff and his attorney to travel to the East Coast to take depositions from the alleged witnesses to the explosions. The defendant decided not to pursue the case, and the judgment in Poole's court stood. Poole was impressed with the attorney for the defense and followed his career closely after that. On occasion, he would drop him a note or write a letter on his behalf. Poole never lost sight of the fact that the legal system dealt with human beings, not just abstract concepts of law.

* * * * *

The issue of trial length is an important one. Before a trial begins, judges try to get estimates about how long it will take. If it goes much longer than the pre-trial estimates, a judge must do all he can to speed it up. There is a saying that justice delayed is justice denied. Poole was always mindful of the calendar, although that rarely did him any good. He recalled that he'd once asked an attorney how long it would take to present his case, and the attorney guessed about two days—and three weeks later he was still presenting his case.

Poole worked hard to stay on top of what was happening in a case. It had been his habit since his days as an assistant district attorney to read the transcript of the day's proceedings each night. "I always insisted on having the police inspectors who were working the case with me get the daily transcript and bring it out to [my house]," he recalled. "The transcript would normally be ready about nine o'clock at night. They'd get out to my house about a quarter of ten. . . . I'd be up until one or two o'clock in the morning going over the transcript and making the notations . . . of what things were of importance, so the next day when I went to court I knew what the evidence was that had already been taken. It was pretty hard on my family because there were a lot of things I didn't do [at home]. But when I was on a trial, I just wasn't available for much of anything else." As a judge on the United States District Court, Poole was nearly always on a trial, so he was nearly always working. "I thought that being a trial judge was what I'd always wanted to be, and I was happy to stay there," he recalled.

Charlotte Poole felt differently. She was sometimes lonely now, especially because she had been forced to cut back on her civic and community activities. Her husband's total immersion in the law and his concentration on one case after another put a definite damper on their evening social life as well as vacation plans.

Charlotte had looked forward to traveling once Patti left home. At her urging, she and Cecil did take some trips abroad. In 1977, they took a tour of the Far East. They flew to Hawaii and from there to Japan, where they visited several cities. From Japan, they flew to Taiwan, then on to Bangkok, Thailand. The following year, Poole returned to East Asia, without Charlotte, as a member of an American Bar Association group invited to visit the People's Republic of China, the mainland communist nation. Also on that trip was Ruth Bader Ginsberg, who would later become the second woman associate justice on the United States Supreme Court. The Chinese had invited the legal group because they wanted to talk about trade, particularly codes for tariffs and for determining allocations of goods and services. Although there was no immediate change in trade relations between mainland China and the United States after that trip, by the 1990s Chinese goods would be as familiar to Americans as Japanese goods had been immediately after World War II.

While he was in China, Poole started having trouble with his sight. On his return home, he went to his doctor. "I was trying a case," Poole later recalled. "I was up there [on the bench] and had a jury coming in, and I was reading the jury the instructions, and all of a sudden I began to see these little wiggles again. I knew the instructions, so I finished them from memory and sent the jury out. Then I went into my chambers and I phoned the ophthalmologist."

Fortunately, the jury reached a verdict the following day, after which Poole went to his doctor, where he learned that both his retinas were detached, and he needed surgery. Two years earlier, he had accidentally bumped into a doorframe at Santa Barbara Airport and been knocked out. According to his doctor, the retinal detachment had probably begun then.

Poole's doctor reserved a room at Children's Hospital (where Charlotte Poole had been vice president of the board of trustees), and Poole was driven there immediately. He was in the hospital for six days. On his release, he still had to wear bandages over his eyes for a couple of weeks. The doctor said the probability of his vision being completely restored was 80 to 85 percent.

Recuperating at home, wearing dark glasses over the bandages on his eyes, Poole went on with his case work. His two law clerks drove out to his house every day and read testimony to him. In the midst of his recovery, Poole got a call from a friend in the U.S. Department of Justice, who told him he was on the short list of nominees for a position on the Ninth Circuit Court of Appeals.

Not long after assuming office in early 1977, President Jimmy Carter had created a committee to identify a group of qualified potential federal court of appeals judges. These judges preside over the appeal of judgments, part of the American legal system's process for redress if a party in a case feels that he or she did not get justice. Appeals of verdicts in U.S. District Court are made in the Circuit Court of Appeals. For the U.S. District Court, Northern District of California, that court is the U.S. Court of Appeals for the Ninth Circuit. The United States is divided geographically into twelve judicial circuits, including the District of Columbia. Each circuit has a court of appeals. Each of the fifty states is assigned to one of the circuits, and the territories are assigned variously to the first, third, and ninth circuits. There is also a Court of Appeals for the Federal Circuit, which has nationwide jurisdiction defined by subject matter.

Several months earlier, at the urging of his friend William Coblentz, Poole had filled out a questionnaire distributed by President Carter's committee. He was not, however, very interested in being an appellate judge. As he later explained, "I was just as content as I could be [on the district court]. I didn't think I was a great legal scholar, and I didn't think that I was going to redo the appellate thinking of the country, and I liked what I was doing." In fact, he had put the application in a drawer. Only after both his friend and his wife nagged him about it did he finally fill out the form just before the submission deadline. In due time, he received a call for an interview. He was aware that one of the goals of the committee—indeed, one of the goals of President Carter in forming the committee—was to expand opportunities for those who had historically been denied them because of race, gender, or religion.

Poole knew that there was a lot of reading to be done as a judge on the Ninth Circuit, and he felt he had to inform the government of his eye surgery. He told the people at the Justice Department that he would know in September whether the surgery had been successful.

In some ways, Poole wanted to use his eye problems as a reason not to ascend to the Ninth Circuit Court of Appeals. He was ambitious, though, and the idea of moving ever upward appealed to him. As Judge Charles Legge put its, "He had a desire to move forward. When he was a lawyer, he wanted to be a prosecutor. As a prosecutor, he wanted to be a judge. As a judge, he wanted to be the next level of judge."

As an appeals judge, he would not preside over trials in a courtroom. Rather he would read trial transcripts and consult the federal statutes and make judgments about whether the law had been followed correctly. He was not familiar with appellate law, and he would have to do a lot of reading and studying to become conversant in it. He preferred being a trial judge. However, there were many pressures on him to accept the higher court job. Charlotte was not the only one who urged him to do so. Many in the black community were eager to see a black judge on the court and saw it as one step away from the United States Supreme Court.

In September, Poole's doctor pronounced his eye surgery successful, Poole informed the Justice Department, and his appointment to the U.S. Court of Appeals for the Ninth Circuit was announced. But once again, it was months before Poole assumed his new position. Says Jerrold Ladar, an assistant U.S. attorney under Poole, "Cecil just would not do things according to schedule. That was his hallmark: whatever the timing was, he'd make up his own."

The delay was not entirely Poole's fault, however. One reason he did not immediately move out of his chambers at the Federal Building on Golden Gate Avenue and into chambers in the building at Seventh and Mission Streets that housed the Ninth Circuit Court judges was that, as he put it, "my chambers were uncertain." The judge who had been his predecessor had occupied gorgeous chambers whose highly polished redwood paneling and gleaming chandeliers were museum quality. In fact, they were so impressive that there was some talk of reserving them as a public viewing space. Poole wanted those chambers. He said half-jokingly, "If you guys don't give me the chambers, I won't ever move."

Chief Judge Marilyn Hall Patel of the U.S. District Court for Northern California says, "I seem to recall that at the same time he was being nominated for the Ninth Circuit, there were also appointments being named for the California Supreme Court. And his name had been sort of bandied about. I said, 'Gosh, I hope they don't nominate him for the supreme court also, because he'll have chambers over at the supreme court, in the Ninth Circuit, and in the district court!'"

Eventually, Chief Judge Richard Chambers relented and allowed Poole to occupy the chambers of his predecessor. Poole moved in, taking several unfinished cases with him from the U.S. District Court. Three or four years later, they were still undecided. Judge Legge recalls, "So the powers that be thought that Cecil should give them up. They were sent back to us and we had to start them all over again. I got one of those cases. But that is the only instance I know of when Cecil didn't do exactly what he should have been doing."

Perhaps Poole hoped that if he completed those unfinished cases, he could burnish his reputation as a district court judge. His tenure on that court had been too short for him to become what Judge William W. Schwarzer, senior judge on the U.S. District Court for the Northern District of California, calls "a significant player" on that court, adding, "He didn't really make much of a record."

Schwarzer continues, "I don't think he was the sort of person who couldn't make up his mind. I just think he let things develop in his mind until he was ready to decide. I don't think he ever felt pressure to get his work out. That wasn't his style. . . . He was a very thoughtful person and he was quite a legal scholar. No one ever questioned the strength of his legal ability and intelligence. In my view, he ruminated over his decisions, and when he felt he was ready he made them."

Judge Thelton Henderson replaced Poole on the district court. He, too, was African American. "That was when I really got to know him," Henderson says, "when I moved into his chambers. He sort of took me under his wing and became my mentor. I was fairly naive about the ways of the legal and judicial world. Cecil knew everything—how things work. He was very helpful. He told me how to get furniture and other things I needed instead of being passive and letting them tell me what I could have. I couldn't have had better guidance. We would have lunch regularly at his favorite place— Original Joe's on Taylor Street. It was an unlikely place. I thought Cecil would be eating at the Banker's Club. He should have been. But everybody knew him there, and I'd get my spaghetti and meatballs and he'd get his calamari. We went over there fairly regularly. Cecil and I could talk about white folks and black folks and how the world was."

Poole also encouraged Henderson to talk about the cases that were before the district court. Those cases interested him, and in the times when he allowed himself to feel regret, he regretted leaving the trial court. It was where he had wanted to be since junior high school.

Judge Fern Smith recalls that Poole put being on that court into perspective for her: "I met him at a very special time of my life, because I had just become a federal judge. It was 1988, and I was having my induction. Typically, the chief judge of the Ninth Circuit comes to the induction of district judges. Whoever it was couldn't come that day, so Cecil came as the designated judge from the court of appeals. The induction was held in the ceremonial courtroom in San Francisco, which is a fairly impressive room. He gave a somewhat typical and traditional welcome. But then he turned around and looked up at me. He was down in the well of the courtroom and I was sitting up on the dais with the rest of my colleagues. And Cecil turned around, and looked up at me, and shook his finger at me, and said, 'And don't you ever forget you've got the best damned job in the whole damned world.' There must have been 200 people there! And he was right, that's exactly what I had. And I've never forgotten it. And after that I felt somewhat of a bond with Cecil. On days when things didn't go as well as I wished they had. Or I got cranky with the lawyers. Or a plaintiff representing himself would come in, not really understand the rules, take more time than I wanted to spend. Well, that was when I remembered what Cecil had said. That I had the best job in the world."

U.S. Circuit Judge Poole cannot resist cutting up at an otherwise august portrait sitting of the members of the U.S. Court of Appeals for the Ninth Circuit, 1980s.

CHAPTER 11

U.S. CIRCUIT JUDGE POOLE

ONCE SETTLED IN HIS IMPRESSIVE CHAMBERS, POOLE STROVE to understand just what he had gotten himself into. At age sixty-five he had achieved the upper reaches of the American judicial system. In the same year as Poole was elevated to the Ninth Circuit Court of Appeals, Sandra Day O'Connor of Arizona became an associate justice on the United States Supreme Court, that court's first female member. Like Justice O'Connor, Poole was a trailblazer. He had compiled an amazing record of "firsts": first black this, first black that. Looking back, he could remember so clearly how isolated he and Charlotte had felt when they had first arrived in San Francisco, how few blacks occupied positions other than janitor or maid, how hostile most whites were to the unwanted newcomers of color. They had come so far.

But sometimes Poole must have felt "lonely at the top." Says his friend Judge Thelton Henderson, "He had tremendous self-control.

It is not surprising. After all those firsts, to essentially be isolated from the black community while he was doing it. And getting the pressures of being black. He was always conscious of setting a standard. He always said that there was nothing he would do to close a door for a black who was coming behind. He was always opening the door by doing a good job. That is a lot of pressure."

The Ninth Circuit Court has jurisdiction over a vast expanse of the western United States. All of Alaska, Arizona, California, Hawaii, Idaho, Montana, Nevada, Oregon, and Washington State are within its boundaries. The twenty-eight judges of the court reside throughout the nine western states in the circuit. The court, with headquarters in San Francisco, sits to hear cases in panels of three judges. Since it is a circuit court, the judges travel. Panels assemble for one week each month in four fixed locations: Seattle, Portland, San Francisco, and Pasadena. Periodically, panels also sit in Alaska, Hawaii, and other districts throughout the circuit. After the hearings, the judges return to their home chambers to write opinions about each case, which are then circulated to the other judges on the panel. Opinions are released by the clerk's office in San Francisco. Jokes Patti Poole, "My father used to love to travel. Before he went onto the circuit court, he'd been bitten by the travel bug. But he stopped liking it when he had to do it as a judge."

The cases that come before the Ninth Circuit Court are many and varied. Most concern the minutiae of the law, and Poole did not find them all that interesting. During an interview with Poole in 1993 for an oral history for the Regional Oral History Program at the University of California, Berkeley, the interviewer showed him ten bound volumes of his opinions. He remarked, "Some of them are worth looking at, and some of them are not. Most of them I don't remember anymore."

In the 1980s, Poole was a member of the three-judge panel that reviewed the 365-year sentence imposed on convicted spy Jerry Whitworth. In 1987, he sat in judgment on a case concerning Supplemental Security Income benefits; in 1988, on a critical state political reapportionment case. The following year, an earthquake severely damaged the San Francisco headquarters of the Ninth Circuit Court, and the court had to move to temporary quarters. In 1990, Poole participated in a decision upholding limits on donations to political campaigns; and in 1994, he was involved in a key ruling on voter representation for Mexican citizens.

Since Congress was continually passing laws, Poole had to keep abreast of the latest legislation and how it affected the cases he was hearing. Among the new laws that had a direct bearing on many of the cases he heard were sentencing guidelines. These provided for minimum sentences for particular crimes—usually after previous convictions.

Laws were not the only things that were new. Before the outbreak of the disease that came to be known as AIDS (Acquired Immune Deficiency Syndrome) in 1981, cases involving the rights of disease carriers were rare. Poole's first AIDS case was the 1988 *Vincent L. Chalk v. United States District*. Chalk, the plaintiff, had been teaching hearing-impaired students in the Orange County schools for approximately six years when he was diagnosed with AIDS in February 1987. In April, after eight weeks of treatment, his personal physician declared him fit to return to work. But in those early days of the AIDS crisis, many people did not understand that the disease cannot be transmitted by casual contact. Some in the school district feared that Chalk might infect his students. He was removed from the classroom and assigned to write grant requests. Chalk sued the school board, but his reassignment was upheld in United States District Court, which held that Chalk, who was being paid the same salary in his reassigned job, was no worse off than before the reassignment.

Every judge who heard the case, and every attorney who represented either side, had to do a lot of reading about AIDS. The main issues to be decided were: (1) whether Chalk was in danger of transmitting the virus to children; and (2) whether the school board had violated his Constitutional rights by reassigning him to a non-teaching position.

When a three-judge panel on the Ninth Circuit Court of Appeals heard a case, one judge wrote the panel's opinion. Poole wrote this one. It was long and intricate, but these were his basic conclusions: In the panel's ruling against Chalk, Poole wrote that the district court had "failed to consider the nature of the alternative work offered Chalk. Chalk's original employment was teaching hearing-impaired children in a small-classroom setting, a job for which he developed special skills beyond those normally required to become a teacher. His closeness to his students and his participation in their lives is a source of tremendous personal satisfaction and joy to him and of benefit to them. The alternative work to which he is now assigned is preparing grant proposals. This job is 'distasteful' to Chalk, involves no student contact, and does not utilize his skills, training or experience. Such non-monetary deprivation is a substantial injury which the court was required to consider.

"Nonetheless, we recognize that the parties and the district court will have to deal with the apprehensions of other members of the school community, as well as with the inexorable progress of Chalk's disease. Although the time frame is unpredictable, given the current state of medical knowledge, the course of petitioner's condition is reasonably certain. Chalk's immune system will deteriorate over time, leaving him increasingly susceptible to opportunistic infections. These infections do not cause AIDS, nor do they increase the risk of transmission of the AIDS virus, but some of them may themselves be communicable to others in a classroom setting. The district court is in the best position, guided by qualified medical opinion, to determine what reasonable procedures, such as periodic reports from petitioner's doctors, will best give assurance to the Department, the community and the court that no significant risk of harm will arise in the future from Chalk's continued presence in the classroom."

This was one of the cases Poole would remember, because a real question of humanity was at stake. Chalk was a man who wanted to teach children, and the school district, out of fear of a new and mysterious disease, had ordered him to leave the classroom. Thus he had been deprived of his rights. On the other hand, his condition damaged his immune system and made him susceptible to infections that might be contagious. His students and other people with whom he came into contact had a right not to be exposed to contagious diseases. The legal issues in such a case could be as intricate as they were in anti-trust cases, but to Poole they were far more interesting because they had a direct and immediate impact on people.

Judge Legge recalled writing an opinion in a California voting rights case that was appealed to the Ninth Circuit. Poole was on the appellate panel and wrote the opinion, overturning a portion of Legge's decision. "Cecil reversed a certain part of that [opinion I wrote]," Legge remembered, "with a very compassionate statement in respect to minorities, saying, essentially, let's look beyond the language of the act and the strict law and see what it looks like in human beings."

Keeping the human aspects of the law in mind went along with Poole's down-to-earth manner. He had little patience with pomp and loved to deflate egos, nearly always in a humorous way, although the humor was sometimes lost on his victims. Says Judge Marilyn Patel, "We were at a Ninth Circuit conference and a senator from a western state was one of the speakers. The guy did not know his audience at all. He was giving this rousing law and order speech, and it struck me that it was not advanced enough. It was the kind you would give to high school students or to the rotary club, and here his audience was all these lawyers and judges. When it came time for questions, Cecil got up and with a perfectly straight face asked the senator, 'Senator, when do you think the Senate will get around to repealing the Fourth Amendment?' The senator replied that he didn't think they'd get around to it this term, but maybe next term. We were just laughing."

This was a two-part joke. One was that Poole considered this particular senator so rabidly law and order that he probably disapproved of the Fourth Amendment, which protects citizens against unreasonable search and seizure. The second part of the joke is that the United States Senate cannot repeal Constitutional amendments, a fact that this particular senator had apparently forgotten.

Judge Charles Renfrew, who served with Poole on the district court, says, "Sitting as a fellow judge with Cecil, [I know] he was a man who had a sense of justice and also a sense of the law, in that one followed the laws and that the law gave predictability to relationships and to transactions, and it was important that everybody just not do what they personally thought was best, but that they do what the law requires, too. A lot of people would say that because Cecil was an Afro-American he was going to think a certain way. But Cecil was going to follow the law, and if the law says something, he's going to follow it. . . . Now if he had discretion, he could do something—you *bet* he'd be sensitive to the concerns of people and interested in doing his thing. He believed in the law. It was a passion for him."

Many of the cases required intensive study of the tiniest details of the law—anti-trust cases, for example, or cases in which he had to decide whether state courts or federal courts had jurisdiction. Poole read transcripts, pored over law books, and studied cases that might serve as precedents. Charlotte complained that he was never home.

By 1982, the Pooles had decided to move across the Golden Gate Bridge to Novato in Marin County. Patti had moved to Marin County in 1976, while she studied at the University of California, Berkeley. Charlotte disliked being alone in the San Francisco house so much, especially at night. She wanted a house that required less maintenance and was easier to negotiate. She also wanted to move to a warmer climate. Reluctant to move at first, Poole finally gave in to his wife's wishes, and they purchased a house in the Marin Country Club Estates in the city of Novato, where Charlotte could renew her love of golf and gardening and swim in the family's pool.

After contracting pneumonia in 1989, Charlotte was diagnosed with lung cancer. When her health declined precipitously later that year, Patti moved into her parents' home to help care for her mother. Patti brought her infant daughter, Nicholle Charlotte Allair, along with her and took a job as a bartender because the hours were flexible. She nursed her mother as long as she could before home care workers took over. Charlotte passed away on February 21, 1991, having achieved her wish to see her granddaughter turn two years old. After her death, Patti and her daughter stayed on in the house with Cecil for about six months. "I think that was the beginning of his decline," she says. "He didn't know what to do without my mom, and I think he felt really guilty because he thought he hadn't told her how much he appreciated her. They were together for fifty years."

"They were such a beautiful couple," says Judge Charles Renfrew. "And Charlotte was a very special woman. . . . In all the turmoil and crisis and amazing things he did in his life, she was always there. She was a steadying force, an anchor. It's hard to describe their relationship, but it was one of mutual love and support, and as a couple they were just greater than the sum of their parts. . . . Cecil had always been kind of a force—he had that kind of personality. But I will tell you there was a marked change in that man's life after he lost Charlotte. I don't think he ever fully recovered from her loss because she was such an important part of his life."

* * * * *

When Charlotte Poole died in February 1991, Cecil Poole was seventy-six, well past retirement age for most people. But federal judges have lifetime tenure; there is no mandatory retirement age for them. Most judges choose to assume senior status, which means that they essentially retire but are able to sit in on cases if they wish. Poole had no interest in taking senior status. The law and Charlotte had been his life, and now Charlotte was gone. So he continued to sit as a circuit judge.

Poole had another reason for not wanting to retire. He wanted to make sure his replacement would be a member of a minority group. Says Patti Poole, "He wanted Thelton Henderson to replace him, but they said Thelton was too old. Dad kept saying that Thelton was the same age that he was when he was appointed to the court. But I think Dad had received a special waiver of the usual age limitation from the ABA, allowing his nomination to go forward. I think he was sixty-one and the cutoff age was sixty."

Poole continued his work. In 1994, he heard a case concerning payment of benefits to a man who had injured his knee while working aboard a tugboat. In 1995, he was one of a three-judge panel that decided a case dealing with the Hopi and Navajo tribes' respective rights to lands in northeastern Arizona.

Meanwhile, Poole faced mounting pressure to retire. Recalls Judge Marilyn Patel, who never forgot that Poole was the first person to welcome her to the Ninth Circuit, "I said to Thelton, 'You know those 30-day final eviction notices? We could get an eviction notice and nail it to his door.'"

At last, Poole gave in. On Martin Luther King, Jr.'s birthday, January 15, 1996, he formally assumed senior status. Coincidentally, just one week before, Willie L. Brown, Jr., had been sworn in as San Francisco's first black mayor. Despite the urgency for Poole to assume senior status, his place on the court remained vacant for more than four years. Not until March 2000 did the United States Senate confirm another minority person—a Latino—Richard A. Paez, on the Ninth Circuit Court of Appeals. As a senior judge, Poole continued to go into his office as often as he could. A driver ferried him back and forth. His secretary accompanied him to appointments and evening affairs.

Senior Judge Cecil Francis Poole died on November 12, 1997, of complications from pneumonia after a long illness. He was eighty-three years old and had spent nearly sixty of those years in the American legal system. He had lived a life in the law, and for much of that life he was a pioneer. He grew up in a time when there were few black people in the legal profession and made his way up to the highest levels of that profession with great dignity and forbearance. When he encountered barriers to advancement, he kept whatever bitter and despairing thoughts he may have had to himself. Says his friend and colleague Judge Charles Legge, "He always kept moving forward without bitterness. I never sensed an angry man there. He was a deep man. I always sensed with Cecil that there were things going on underneath that he wasn't going to share."

Whatever the cost to him personally, by keeping his own counsel and abiding by his own high standards, Poole helped to open doors for blacks and other minorities. But his legacy is much more than as a trailblazer for equal opportunity. "He was a force," says friend and colleague Judge Charles Renfrew. "He was a force in the lives of his friends and in the law and in the community. And part of the strength of his force was his adherence to his own high standards of excellence and performance." A jurist who never lost sight of the people whom the law is supposed to serve, Poole also never lost his passion for the law and the standards it represented. Through all the changes in the political and social climate that Poole experienced

Judge Poole and his daughter, Patti, 1990
San Francisco Examiner photo by Chris Hardy

in his lifetime, the law was an anchor. The same can be said for the life of the nation he so long and ably served.

* * * * *

On May 22, 2000, the San Francisco Board of Supervisors declared the Joseph Leonard/Cecil F. Poole House, located at 90 Cedro Avenue, a San Francisco historical landmark.

CHRONOLOGY

1914 (June 28) Serb nationalist assassinates
Archduke Ferdinand of Austria-Hungary

   World War I breaks out in Europe

   (July 25) Cecil F. Poole born

1915 Ku Klux Klan reorganizes

1917 United States officially declares war on Germany

1918 Poole family migrates from Birmingham, Alabama,
to Pittsburgh, Pennsylvania

1927 Aviator Charles Lindbergh flies *The Spirit of St. Louis*
nonstop from New York to Paris

1932 Poole enters the University of Michigan

1936 Poole earns B.A. from the University of Michigan

1938 Poole earns law degree from the University of Michigan

1939 Poole earns master's degree in law from Harvard University

   World War II begins

1940 Poole passes the Pennsylvania bar

   Poole is denied membership in the American Bar Association

1941   Poole joins the National Labor Relations Board
       United States enters World War II

1942   Poole is drafted into the United States Army
       Poole marries Charlotte Crump

1945   World War II ends

1946   Poole is honorably discharged from the army; he and
       Charlotte relocate to San Francisco; Poole gets a job
       with the Office of Price Administration

1947   Gayle Alexandra Poole is born

1949   Poole goes to work as an assistant district attorney in the
       office of District Attorney Edmund G. "Pat" Brown

1950   Brown is elected attorney general of California

1952   Patricia Mary Poole is born

1954   United States Supreme Court rules in *Brown v. Board
       of Education* that "separate but equal" education
       is unconstitutional

1955   Rosa Parks is arrested on a segregated bus in Montgomery,
       Alabama; Montgomery bus boycott follows

1958   Edmund "Pat" Brown is elected governor of California;
       appoints Poole his extradition and clemency secretary

1960   (May 2) Caryl Chessman is executed

1961 (June 29) Poole is appointed by President John F. Kennedy as U.S. attorney for the Northern District of California—first black U.S. attorney in the continental United States

1963 (November 22) President John F. Kennedy is assassinated

1964 Federal Civil Rights Act is passed

(December) Poole is denied a seat on the NAACP Board of Directors

1965 Federal Voting Rights Act is passed

President Lyndon B. Johnson appoints Thurgood Marshall the first black solicitor general of the United States

1966 Poole joins the American Bar Association

Black Panther Party for Self-Defense is formed

1967 President Johnson appoints Thurgood Marshall the first black justice on the U.S. Supreme Court

Anti-draft and anti-war demonstrations occur across the country

1968 (April) Martin Luther King, Jr., is assassinated

(June) Robert F. Kennedy is assassinated

Poole is nominated to U.S. District Court for Northern California by President Lyndon B. Johnson; Senate fails to confirm and nomination is withdrawn

Richard M. Nixon is elected president

1969 Poole returns to private law practice

1972   President Nixon resigns; Vice President Gerald R. Ford
        assumes the presidency

1976   President Ford appoints Poole to the U.S. District Court
        for the Northern District of California

1979   President Jimmy Carter appoints Poole to the
        U.S. Court of Appeals for the Ninth Circuit

1991   Charlotte Crump Poole dies

1996   (January 15) Poole assumes senior judge status

1997   (November 12) Cecil F. Poole dies of complications
        from pneumonia after a long illness

2000   (May 22) San Francisco Board of Supervisors declares
        90 Cedro Avenue the Joseph Leonard/Cecil F. Poole House,
        city landmark number 213.

BIBLIOGRAPHY

Books

Bodnar, John, Roger Simon, and Michael P. Weber. *Lives of Their Own: Blacks, Italians, and Poles in Pittsburgh, 1900-1960.* Urbana and Chicago: University of Illinois Press, 1982.

Haskins, James. *Jesse Jackson: Civil Rights Activist.* Berkeley Heights, NJ: Enslow Publishers, Inc., 2000.

_____. *Power to the People: The Rise and Fall of the Black Panther Party.* New York: Simon and Schuster, 1997.

_____. *Thurgood Marshall: A Life for Justice.* New York: Henry Holt & Co., 1992.

Haskins, James, and Kathleen Benson. *The 60s Reader.* New York: Viking Kestrel, 1988.

Hicke, Carole. *Civil Rights, Law, and the Federal Courts: The Life of Cecil Poole, 1914-1997.* Northern California U.S. District Court Oral History Series. Berkeley: The Regents of the University of California, 1997.

Lewis, David Levering. *W. E. B. Du Bois: The Fight for Equality and the American Century.* New York: Henry Holt & Co., 2000.

Parks, Rosa, with Jim Haskins. *Rosa Parks: My Story.* New York: Dial Books, 1992.

Seale, Bobby. *Seize the Time: The Story of the Black Panther Party and Huey P. Newton.* New York: Random House, 1970.

Articles and Other Sources

Burlingame Advance Star. April 14, 1963.

"Cecil Poole Returns to S.F." *San Francisco Examiner.* June 9, 1961, p. 8.

Fleming, Thomas C. "Carlton B. Goodlett, Champion of the People," *Columbus Free Press,* June 4, 1999. n.p.

Poole, Cecil F. "The Negro and Equal Justice," speech to the Commonwealth Club, Sheraton-Palace Hotel, San Francisco, July 1, 1963.

"Poole to be UC Professor, 'Not Bitter' Over U.S. Job." *San Francisco Examiner.* December 13, 1969. n.p.

Transcript of Induction Ceremony of Honorable Cecil F. Poole, Judge, The United States District Court, Northern District of California, Tuesday, October 5, 1976, San Francisco, California.

Index

ABOUT THE AUTHOR

JAMES HASKINS GREW UP IN BIRMINGHAM, ALABAMA, CECIL Poole's birthplace. As a boy, he could not enter the segregated public library. His first book, *Diary of a Harlem Schoolteacher*, recounted his experience teaching special education students in New York City. Mr. Haskins started writing for children and young adults when he realized there were not enough books on current events for his students to read. He has now published more than one hundred books, many of which can now be found in the same public library that he was barred from entering as a boy. Mr. Haskins has won wide acclaim for his writing, and is a three-time recipient of the Coretta Scott King Award. He is Professor of English at the University of Florida, Gainesville. He continues to be interested in the people from his hometown.

THE NINTH JUDICIAL CIRCUIT HISTORICAL SOCIETY

FOUNDED IN 1985, THE NINTH JUDICIAL CIRCUIT HISTORICAL Society is dedicated to preserving our legal heritage and educating the public about the fundamental importance of our judicial system. The non-profit organization takes its name from the United States Courts for the Ninth Circuit, the federal court circuit that serves nine states in the American West and the Pacific Islands. In addition to publishing books, the NJCHS publishes the scholarly journal *Western Legal History*, prepares traveling exhibits, and records oral histories of prominent judges and lawyers. Through its outreach program, the NJCHS has distributed its *Bill of Rights* learning guide to over 450 schools.

The Ninth Judicial Circuit Historical Society
125 South Grand Avenue
Pasadena, California 91105

THE JUDGE CECIL POOLE
BIOGRAPHY PROJECT

THIS PROJECT IS A PART OF THE NJCHS COMMUNITY OUTREACH program. We believe that Judge Poole's life is a model, especially for today's young people to emulate. The project is divided into three phases: 1) the preservation of Judge Poole's personal papers; 2) the researching and writing of Judge Poole's biography for young adult readers; 3) the publishing and distribution of the book to secondary schools and youth centers. The project has been funded by grants from foundations and other groups and contributions from more than 200 individuals.